Design an Expandable House
For Present Needs and Future Dreams

Second Edition

by Stanley Mazor

Design an Expandable House
For Present Needs and Future Dreams

Second Edition

by Stanley Mazor

Unlimited Publishing
Bloomington Indiana

Copyright © 2006 by Stanley Mazor

Cover design by Charles King and Rob Cheng. Book design by Stanley Mazor and Charles King. Photographs used with permission from Stanley Mazor, Steven Banks, Don Murray, Kathleen Reeve, Julie Haber, Greg Wahl-Stephens. "Vendors' Comments" text used with permissions from Don Murray, Elvin Spurling, Pete Hedenstrom, Karl Holik, and Steven Banks.

All rights reserved under Title 17, U.S. Code, International and Pan-American Copyright Conventions. No part of this work, whether in printed or digital form, may be reproduced or transmitted in any form or by any means, electronic or mechanical, including (but not limited to) photocopying, scanning, recording, live performance or broadcast, or duplication by any information storage or retrieval system without prior written permission from the author(s) and publisher(s).

Unlimited Publishing LLC ("UP") works with professional authors and publishers, serving as distributing publisher. Sole responsibility for the content of each work rests with the author(s) and/or co-publisher(s). Information or opinions expressed herein may not be interpreted as originating from, or endorsed by UP, nor any of its officers, members, contractors, agents or assigns.

This book is publicly offered contingent on the reader's prior understanding that any medical, health, legal, investment or other professional advice of any kind should be independently confirmed by a qualified source. The author(s) and publisher(s) accept no responsibility of any kind for conclusions reached by readers of this book. If you do not agree with these terms, you may return this book in good condition for a full refund.

This second edition revises and replaces the first edition, published in 2003.

Second Edition

ISBN 978-1-58832-234-0

Contributing Publisher: Stanley Mazor

Distributing Publisher:

Unlimited Publishing LLC

http://www.unlimitedpublishing.com

Table of Contents

Acknowledgements v

Foreword xi

Chapter 1---Inspiration and Overview 1-1

Chapter 2---The Design 2-1

Chapter 3---Land and Site Planning 3-1

Chapter 4---Foundation and Building Materials 4-1

Chapter 5---Construction Phases 5-1

Chapter 6---Vendor's Comments 6-1

Alan Miller, Miller's Renaissance Landscape Design 6-1
Don Murray, Site Preparation 6-2
Elvin Spurling, Western Design 6-3
Pete Hedenstrom, Rastra Rep 6-4
Steven Banks, General Contractor 6-5
Karl Holik, Rastra Corporation 6-6

Afterword---Looking Back and Forth 6-8

About the Author 6-9

Reader Exercises 6-10

Appendix ---Vendors 6-11

Acknowledgements

An amateur like myself can only succeed because of the experiences, skill and craftsmanship of the many artisans who worked on this project. Western Design, the firm that did the detailed drawings, has a motto: "If you can dream it, we can design it." The engineering firm KAS and Associates made a multitude of decisions on the materials, such as using steel beams in the garage and tower, and performed numerous engineering computations.

My contractor, Steven Banks of Northwestern Hand Crafted Homes, has many years of successful custom home construction and is not only a skilled craftsman in his own right, but is also backed by a variety of skilled subcontractors. The framers and carpenters, including Richard Olney, Marshall Foltz, Gary Arras and Doug Workman, created a work of art. The plumbers, electricians, plasterers, painters, and others were experienced craftsmen who made the project successful. I had the dream, but a skilled team of craftsman made it a reality.

Thanks to Don Murray, Bill Hicks and Rick Hartwein for site development; to Carolyn Allman, Marlys Weinman, Paula Sendar and Nola Ohara for interior designs and colors, Joi Shannon and Steven LaRose for stencil work, and to M. C. Chan and D. Siljak for interior design. Andrew Young and Steve Borlik at Young and Borlik, Architects, Palo Alto suggested the long horizontal axis. Susan Englestein planned the rear landscape.

Manuscript review: Flo Pallakoff, Sandra Goldstein, Mike Korn, Maurine Mazor.
Editing: Mary Eisenhart, Charles King, and Dan Snow.

Photo credits are: Kathleen Reeve, Greg Wahl-Stephens and Julie Haber.
Cover design: Charles King and Rob Cheng

List of Figures

Figure 1-1a: Norman chateau front view
Figure 1-1b: Norman chateau front view close-up
Figure 1-2a: Taking measurements in Normandy
Figure 1-2b: Norman chateau far perspective view
Figure 1-3a: Chateau Herbe phase 1 front view
Figure 1-3b: Chateau Herbe front elevation
Figure 1-4: Chateau Herbe sequential front elevations
Figure 1-5a: Chateau Herbe 1st floor plan - center
Figure 1-5b: 900 sq. ft. subset floor plan
Figure 1-5c: 500 sq. ft. subset floor plan
Figure 1-6a: View of a garage
Figure 1-6b: Perspective view of garage
Figure 1-7a: Block wall close-up view
Figure 1-7b: View of Arizona construction site
Figure 1-8a: Herbe phase 2 garage end and front view
Figure 1-8b: Herbe phase 2 garage end and rear view

Figure 2-1a: Chateau Herbe front elevation
Figure 2-1b: Chateau Herbe 1st floor plan
Figure 2-2a: Floor plan for center section 1st floor
Figure 2-2b: View of front door from foyer
Figure 2-3a: Norman chateau rear center view
Figure 2-3b: Chateau Herbe rear center view
Figure 2-4a: Norman chateau front center view
Figure 2-4b: Chateau Herbe front center view
Figure 2-5a: View of foyer stairwell and kitchen
Figure 2-5b: View at bottom of stairway
Figure 2-6a: Foyer L-stairway plan
Figure 2-6b: Stairwell plan and elevation
Figure 2-7a: U-stairwell perspective drawing
Figure 2-7b: U-stairwell floor plan
Figure 2-8: Third floor bedroom floor plan

Figure 3-1a: Sample topographic map
Figure 3-1b: Ashland home site view
Figure 3-2: Draft site plan
Figure 3-3a: Water wellhead
Figure 3-3b: View of creek side boundary
Figure 3-4a: View of elevated building pad
Figure 3-4b: View of driveway from pad
Figure 3-5a: View of septic tank near house
Figure 3-5b: View of phase 2 from tree-lined driveway
Figure 3-6a: Perspective of phase 2 garage end

Figure 3-6b: View of phase 2 site from rear lawn
Figure 3-7a: Measuring sun trajectory at site
Figure 3-7b Recording sun trajectory on site plan
Figure 3-8: View of phase 2 through vineyard

Figure 4-1a View of foundation piers
Figure 4-1b: View of grade beam rebar connections
Figure 4-2a: View of poured grade beam in forms
Figure 4-2b: View of first course blocks
Figure 4-3: Designer's sample floor plan
Figure 4-4a: View of foam block delivery
Figure 4-4b: View of phase 2 block framing
Figure 4-5a: View of interior block wall
Figure 4-5b: View of joists at ledger beam
Figure 4-6a: View of line pump for blocks
Figure 4-6b: View of overhead pump
Figure 4-7a: View of electric wiring within block wall
Figure 4-7b: View of cabinet supports within block wall
Figure 4-8a: View of prefab arch in doorway
Figure 4-8b: View of front stucco application
Figure 4-9a: View of arched window installation
Figure 4-9b: View of rear deck balustrade
Figure 4-10a: View of rear second floor deck
Figure 4-10b: Corbel profile pattern
Figure 4-10c: View of tower fascia box and corbels

Figure 5-1a: Front view during phase 2
Figure 5-1b: View of phase 1 blocks
Figure 5-2: View of third floor framing
Figure 5-3a: First floor plan for phase 1
Figure 5-3b: View of phase 1 foyer/kitchen
Figure 5-4a: View of rear porch
Figure 5-4b: View of phase 2 garage
Figure 5-5a: First floor plan
Figure 5-5b: Second floor plan
Figure 5-6: View of study ceiling beams
Figure 5-7a: View of phase 2 front
Figure 5-7b: View of rear tower corbels
Figure 5-8a: View of steel tripod
Figure 5-8b: View of tower construction
Figure 5-9a: View of rear tower
Figure 5-9b: View of steel deck support
Figure 5-10a: View of phase 3 right wing
Figure 5-10b: Rear view of right wing
Figure 5-11a: Floor plan right wing --original
Figure 5-11b: Floor plan right wing --revised

Figure 5-12a: View of right wing framing
Figure 5-12b: View of living room steel ceiling joists
Figure 5-13a: View of rear nook and dining room
Figure 5-13b: View of Chateau during phase 4
Figure 5-14a: View of living room door panels
Figure 5-14b: View of living room fireplace and cabinets
Figure 5-15a: View of study end wall
Figure 5-15b: View of third floor tower interior
Figure 5-16a: View of third floor tower rear window
Figure 5-16b: View of door and window moldings
Figure 5-17a: View of bathroom cabinet and moldings
Figure 5-17b: Mazors in the finished study
Figure 5-18a: View of breaking-thru to existing building
Figure 5-18b: View of exterior thermal profile

Figure 6-1a: Photo of Skinner and Miller
Figure 6-1b: Photo of Spurling and Banks
Figure 6-2: View of tripod installation
Figure 6-3a: View of foyer kitchen
Figure 6-3b: View of rear deck scupper spout
Figure 6-4a: S. Banks and R. Olney sawing 30" block
Figure 6-4b: Framing with block
Figure 6-5a: View of concrete pouring
Figure 6-5b: Close-up view of concrete in block
Figure 6-6a: Mazors toast in Garden Room
Figure 6-6b: View of phase 4 construction

Foreword

"A man's home is his castle." But what if he wants a castle for a home?

Many people strive to create enduring artistic works. To me, a beautiful building is such a work. I've been overwhelmed by the splendor of classic European buildings that have survived for centuries. With that inspiration, and taking advantage of modern-day improvements in methods and materials, I embarked on my own project: using Styrofoam® building blocks and a modular construction approach to build my own chateau. Today my needs are few, and the structure is small, but I dream of having a "grand villa" someday (and perhaps converting it into an inn or B&B). In the process of "growing a chateau," I hope to create an aesthetically pleasing building that serves as an inspiration to others.

In the spirit of such works as *Mr. Blandings Builds His Dream House* and *Under the Tuscan Sun*, I wrote this book about the experience of designing and constructing my expandable home, not only to chronicle the experience but to serve as a resource for the aspiring designer. Each time you turn the page, you'll find a photo or diagram to illustrate the point being discussed. Whether your taste in architecture runs, like mine, to neoclassical Norman chateaux, or to another style, this book will give you some useful ideas and help you avoid some pitfalls.

This second edition was written in 2006 after completing the right wing; it revises, corrects, and extends the 2003 edition.

Disclaimer and caveat: I am neither a lawyer nor an architect. While this book documents the experiences and lessons acquired in the course of my own project, it is not intended as a substitute for professional advice.

Ashland, Oregon — 2006

Figure 1-1a: Norman chateau front view

Figure 1-1b: Norman chateau front view close-up

Chapter 1
Inspiration and Overview

After studying French in high school and taking several business trips and vacations in France, I became attracted to the remarkable architecture of the old chateaux. Some are true fortified castles, but many are just large villas. Since over 20,000 chateaux were built in France, they are relatively easy to locate, and many have been converted to hotels or museums that are open to the public.

Over the years I've collected books with photos and details of these big houses. One such book features the chateau shown in Figure 1-1a, built in Normandy in the 17th century. It has a central foyer and two wings; there's a large tower on the left and a narrow, shorter tower on the right. It was constructed in at least **two phases** over a period of 100 years; the original architect planned a four-tower quadrangle structure, but only one tower was built because the owner ran short of funds. The article explains: "Years later ... a second tower and wing were added."

These two towers provide visual balance, but the structure is not symmetrical, which sets it apart from typical neoclassical architecture of the period. However, the windows are placed symmetrically around the front door, as shown in the close-up photo of the entrance in Figure 1-1b. The article mentions that the house is a mere 16' wide. You can see directly through to the rear portion of the estate from the front windows and doors, as shown in the photo. Although very narrow, the building appears to be about 150' long. This is an unusual footprint by modern standards; today's houses are usually built more square to reduce the cost of the roof and foundation, and to allow more circulation between rooms.

The floor plan of this chateau is not published, but the photos in the book show the interior of three rooms. Old castles often had few hallways; the rooms would simply abut one another. Given the slight 16' width of this building, it seems likely that it too was built without corridors.

The building's unusual shape caused me to wonder how the rooms were arranged. If you were to design a similar chateau with the rooms in a line, what would the floor plan be like? As a game, I tried to find a way of placing the rooms and started drawing some room arrangements on engineering grid paper. Starting with the garage on one end, I tried to put pieces of this puzzle together and wondered about building it in multiple stages, since the original had been built in stages. Is there a way to *grow this chateau* while minimizing the growing pains?

In this book you'll see my answer and approach in building my own chateau using this Norman chateau as my inspiration. But to proceed I needed to know more about the original French chateau.

Note: Figure numbers correspond to the opposing text page.

Figure 1-2a: Taking measurements in Normandy

Figure 1-2b: Norman chateau far perspective view

Normandy Search

I soon wanted more information about this particular French chateau. The book mentions that it's near the city of Deauville, but does not identify its exact location. My sister Debi was going on a vacation to France. As a legal researcher, she's quite expert in getting information, and she volunteered to try to locate this chateau. Her friend Philippe, who owns an antique shop in Paris, was able to get the phone number for the Marquis mentioned in the book as the chateau's owner.

In August 1997 my wife, Maurine, and I took a one-week walking tour of the Dordogne region of France. We extended this trip and spent a weekend on the north coast of France in Honfleur, Normandy, about 30 minutes from the Deauville chateau. Although it is a private residence, we phoned the Marquis, who speaks perfect English, and arranged a visit "just to take some exterior photos"— and to take some measurements of the chateau's exterior. Maurine helped to measure the chateau and acted as a measuring stick, as seen in the front door photo, Figure 1-2a.

The building is about 15% larger than it appeared in the book. The left tower is about 30'; the wing between the tower and the central section is 33'; the center foyer section is 30' long. As shown in the photo in Figure 1-2b, the building is surrounded by a lovely moat, originally built for fortification, and has well manicured lawns and sculpted hedges.

Our visit to France helped me complete my plans for a house that looks similar to the original chateau externally, but has a unique room arrangement and was built in multiple phases. What began as curiosity about an article became the starting point of my new dream house that may someday become an inn.

My building's name, inspired by that of the Norman chateau, is "Herbe II." This book refers to the house simply as "Herbe" (pronounced "Herbie"). It details the incremental design and four construction phases of Chateau Herbe with Insulated Concrete Form (ICF) Styrofoam blocks in Ashland, Oregon during 1999-2005.

During the course of this construction project I considered many variations and changed my mind from time to time. Whereas most books don't reveal the thought process or underlying thinking that went into a project, I'll try to explain some of the options I considered and the final choices I made in the design and construction of Chateau Herbe.

You'll also find a chapter, "Vendors' Comments," giving other perspectives on this project. If you are considering a multi-staged house development, or using Styrofoam building blocks, you might gain some insights from my experiences. Look for the highlighted **Lessons Learned**.

Lessons Learned: Benefit from others' mistakes.

Figure 1-3a: Chateau Herbe phase 1 front view

Figure 1-3b: Chateau Herbe front elevation

Building in Stages

The first phase of Herbe was only 35' wide, as shown in Figure 1-3a, and my neighbors referred to it as "the chateau" because of its neoclassic styling, typical of European villas. My little house would truly deserve this name when it expanded, four times larger, with the addition of the left and right wings, as shown in Figure 1-3b.

Designing a building that could be constructed — and used — in manageable increments was a key goal of this project. My motto is: "Design a home for your present needs and your future dreams." Today's homeowners discover an all-too-common problem when they try to make their current house fit their changing needs: the original floor plan layout of most existing houses severely restricts expansion possibilities; similarly, new home plans offer few expandable designs. This motivated me all the more strongly to pursue my own expandable design.

With Herbe, the goal was **design a large house, then build a small house**, postponing construction of more living space until it's wanted. Hence the chateau, Figure 1-3b, was partitioned into pieces that can be built sequentially. The challenge was to decide how to partition the design and in what order to build the pieces. While this approach is sometimes called "modular construction," that term is more commonly used to refer to the use of pre-built components or "modules"; since we didn't use pre-built modules, I try to avoid this confusing term.

Expandable Design - Pros, Cons, Issues

Not only can an expandable house evolve to accommodate your needs or budget, but you often can get a better final result by working in manageable stages instead of tackling a major design all at once. This process allows you to discover what you want; it also lets you "pay as you go" and minimizes risk. I built the 8,100-square-foot Chateau Herbe in four construction phases over a six-year period. Some of the revisions I made during this extended design period are described in this book.

In multi-phased construction, the hard-won lessons of early phases often yield greater efficiency and cost-effectiveness in later stages. Particularly in projects with "non-standard" aspects — e.g. novel materials or techniques, or special site requirements — the early learning can lead to significant savings later. For example, in the construction of Herbe, it took only 1/6 as much labor to place concrete in the foundation piers during phase 2 as it did in phase 1. Money was saved by re-using a single set of foundation forms for both wings because of the design symmetry. The expensive engineering of the left tower was re-used for the design of the second, right tower. The symmetry will be evident.

On the other hand, building a home in stages is less cost-effective than building it all at one time. Something as simple as matching floor, roof, and foundation lines is easy when you're building a house all at once, but more challenging in a multi-stage project. You lose economy of scale, and each stage generates costs for permits, inspections and subcontractors; additionally, construction is always messy, risky and time-consuming.

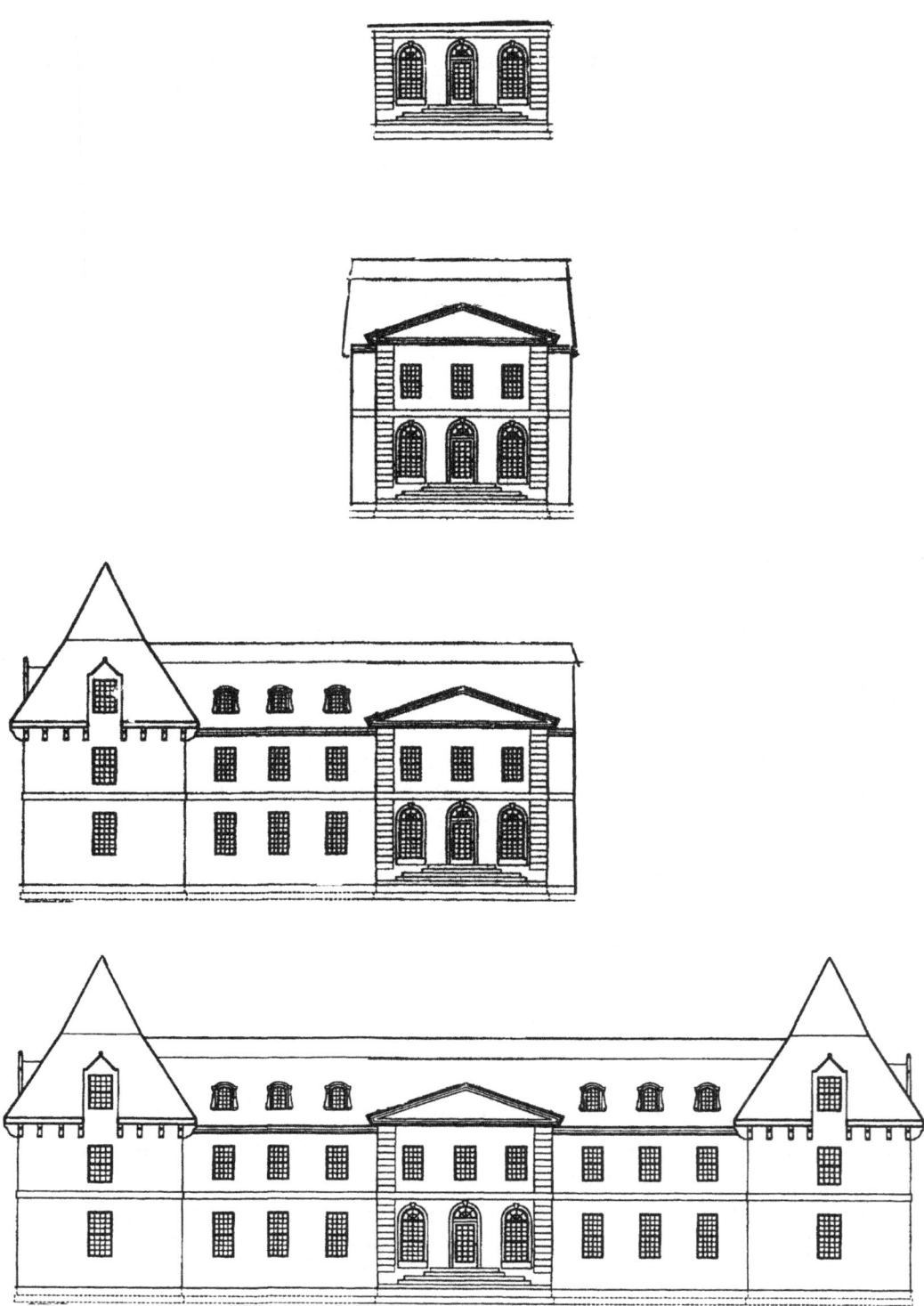

Figure 1-4: Chateau Herbe sequential front elevations

Growing a Chateau
Figure 1-4 illustrates the front elevation view of Herbe as it expands in several construction stages. The top view is just a single-story cottage; my actual phase 1, a three-story, two-bedroom house, is shown below that. Either or both side wings are then added. I added the left wing first because it contains the garage.

Several questions are inherent in multi-stage construction:

- How practical is the house at each stage of development?
- What has to be "thrown away" at each construction stage?
- How can plumbing, electrical, HVAC, entry, and stairs be placed?
- Are the additions built horizontally or vertically?
- What are the extra costs of phased construction?
- How do the local building codes affect the project?

While your requirements may be very different from mine, this book's explanation of the problems encountered, and how they were solved, may save some time and trouble on your own project.

The strategy of designing the entire building, then constructing it in stages, is similar to the way I've been designing computer hardware and software for over 40 years, using a method called "top-down design." In the context of construction, the term doesn't mean "design the roof first"; it means to set overall project goals and include requirements in the original plan to enable the "grand" final result.

The opposite approach, "bottom-up design," also came into play: designing in such a way that the component parts determine the final result. For example, specifying individual room sizes to establish the building's footprint is a bottom-up approach. While an expandable design is best achieved in a top-down manner, that design should take full account of bottom-up issues — for example, my choice of building materials affected the stages in which Herbe would be constructed.

Plan to Change, Expand - And Perhaps Shrink
In its ultimate stage, Chateau Herbe has six or more bedrooms, each with its own private bathroom. This may seem excessive for a private residence, but it's a nice size for a Bed and Breakfast Inn (B&B). If the long-term goal is to operate such a business, it can make sense to live in the building during its early phases, but you need to allow for private access, extra storage space and sound insulation for a B&B. In the Herbe design, the dining room and living room sizes were chosen to be appropriate for a B&B.

By the same token, as a family requires less space, a homeowner might want to "slice and dice" an oversized house into multiple flats. A good top-down design should incorporate downsizing as an option and plan accordingly — for example, having separate entrances and stairways to upstairs rooms. Chapter 5 describes a novel staircase that facilitates separate entrances in my revised Herbe design.

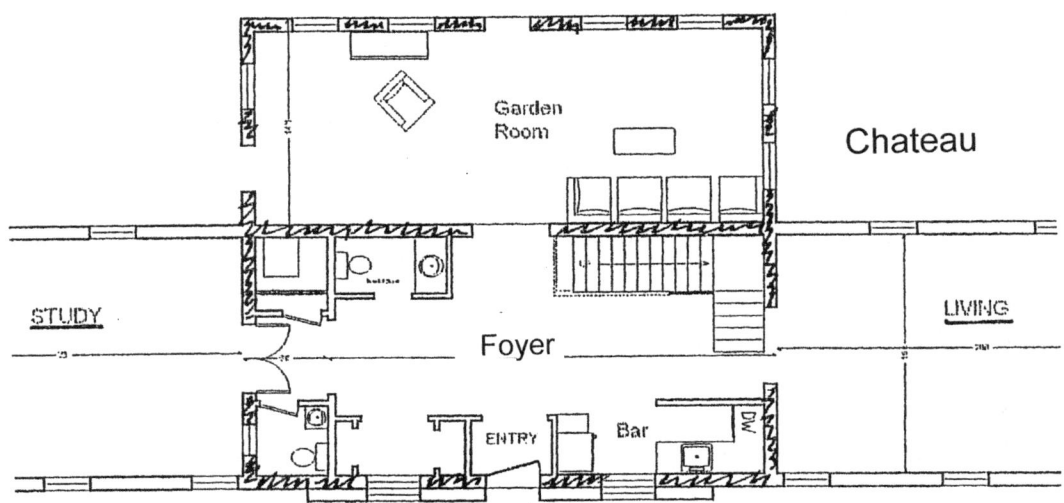

Figure 1-5a: Chateau Herbe 1st floor plan – center

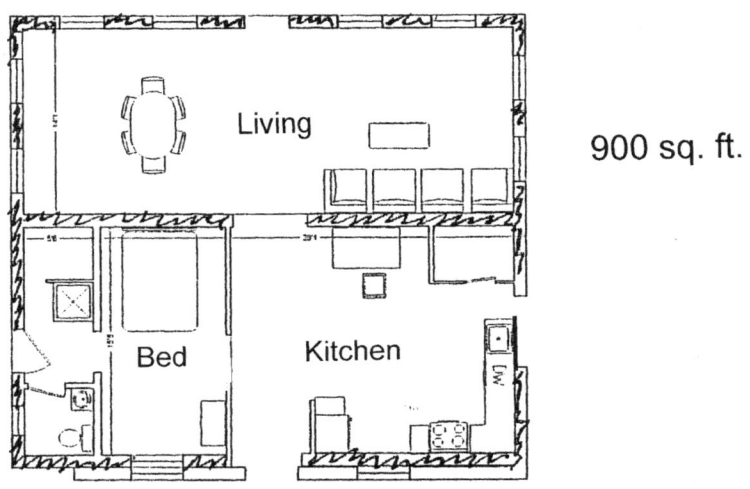

Figure 1-5b: 900 sq. ft. subset floor plan

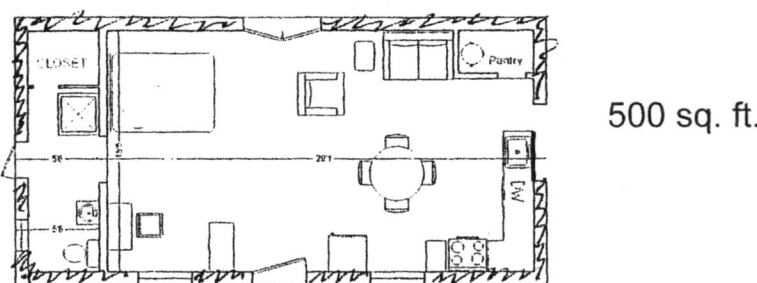

Figure 1-5c: 500 sq. ft. subset floor plan

Multi-Phase Design - Possible Approaches

I designed Herbe to be constructed in six (or fewer) phases, as shown in Table 1. What begins as a 500-square-foot, one-room cottage grows to an 8,000-square-foot, six-bedroom house; the design is discussed in greater detail in Chapter 2. (For practical reasons, the construction of Herbe began with option 4.)

Table 1:
Six Construction Options

	Option	Size-sq. ft.	Stories	Configuration
	1.	500	1	cottage
	2.	900	1	1-bedroom, 1-bath home
	3.	1,350	2	2-bedroom, 2-bath home
->	4.	1,800	3	2-bedroom, 2½-bath home
	5.	4,800	3	5-bedroom, 6-bath home with garage
	6.	8,000	3	6-bedroom Chateau Herbe

Figures 1-5 show the ground-level floor plans for some options in Table 1. Figure 1-5a shows the first floor of the Chateau Herbe (option 6). The upper-level floor plans and the two towers aren't shown here. The garage is in the left tower and a study in the left wing; there's a foyer in the center, with a garden room behind it. The living room, dining room and kitchen are in the right wing. Note that the foyer has a staircase leading above.

In theory, this chateau could be built incrementally from much smaller structures that are **subsets** of the overall design. Figures 1-5b and 1-5c show, respectively, a one-bedroom house (option 2), and a one-room cottage (option 1) that could grow into this chateau. Note the identical placement of the doors and windows in the structure.

900-Square-Foot House

Figure 1-5b shows a floor plan for a one-story, one-bedroom home that can eventually expand into the chateau structure. A proper subset of the chateau plan, with identical exterior wall and window locations, it has a living room in the back and a bedroom and kitchen in the front. An interior wall, included at this stage to separate the bedroom from the kitchen, will be removed in later stages to convert the space to an open foyer. Since this is only a one-story building there is no stairway, but one will be needed later; to facilitate its eventual construction, no walls or plumbing are placed in the future stairwell's location. The current bathroom will become the powder room, and the kitchen becomes the chateau's wet bar, allowing the continued use of plumbing.

500-Square-Foot Cottage

Finally, Figure 1-5c is the floor plan for a small, single-room cottage that is a proper subset of both the chateau and the small house, and that could be the building's starting point. A wall or partition could divide the bedroom and the kitchen at this stage if desired, as in the one-bedroom design. A shower could be used to complete the bathroom. This might be deleted in later stages when only a powder room was needed, or the plumbing might be used to add a laundry.

Figure 1-6a: View of a garage

Figure 1-6b: Perspective view of garage

Another Story

Adding a second story of 450 square feet to either of these small designs provides two more options: 1,350 and 950 square feet (some of which space will be lost to the stairwell). If you choose to build a second story now and a third later, building an exterior flat roof over the two-level structure might facilitate the later construction. A pitched roof would have to be removed and relocated. Since my project started with a three-story building, I have no experience with adding upwards, and you should get expert advice on these choices. It certainly seems like an interesting option.

As you add structures vertically the stairways become very important — what space they take up, and where in the floor plan they access the floor above. Any upwards-expandable design needs to include careful plans for the locations of these stairways; elevators are also interesting to consider as explained in chapter 5.

Lessons Learned: Consider adding up, as well as left/right.

Garage First - An Alternate Approach

As these designs suggest, one natural choice for the first construction phase is the building's core — a kitchen and bathroom. Another approach that has worked well for some people is to build the garage first. Among the benefits: the garage can serve as a workshop and can store building materials as construction progresses. Also, it can provide interim living space.

Figure 1-6 shows such a project, unrelated to my project, a garage with an apartment above (an extra bedroom or apartment on top of a garage might be useful for long-term guests even after the house is built). The covered walkway to the left leads from the garage to the entry door of the future house. Meanwhile, downstairs, there's a temporary living room and a kitchen that will be gutted when the final house is built and this structure is converted to a garage. Some of the current plumbing might be left in place to provide a gardening center or a clean-up sink.

Lessons Learned: Research others' designs.

This approach works best when the garage is a stand-alone building. Because Herbe's garage is in the left tower (Figure 1-4) and because placing the kitchen there didn't work well with the upgrade plan, I didn't take this option. However, after thinking about various options over the years, I've become convinced that I also could have started in the left wing. If you would have asked me about it originally I would have rejected the idea — so I've learned that the garage-first approach has many merits and I wish that I'd given it more consideration.

Lessons Learned: Consider building the garage first.

Figure 1-7a: Block wall close-up view

Figure 1-7b: View of Arizona construction site

Building With Styrofoam Blocks

In the early 1990s, I was in Japan on a business trip. While there I happened to see, stacked 8-12 high in an alley for garbage collection, some rigid Styrofoam packaging materials of the type used to protect consumer electronics in shipping. Seeing this stack made me wonder if it would be possible to build, say, a storage shed or a children's playhouse from Styrofoam construction blocks, reinforced with wooden 2"x4"s.

Upon my return to the U.S., I discovered, to my surprise, that Styrofoam building blocks were already in commercial use. I immediately wanted to know more about the form factor of the blocks, how they're made and how they're being used.

In 1997, my wife and I toured a home being constructed in Arizona to learn more about these blocks, and some photos from our trip are in Figure 1-7. In this single-story building, the foam blocks are glued together to form the exterior walls. The seams are visible. There are 6" holes in the block for forming poured concrete columns, the structural support for the building walls, as the blocks are actually forms for placing the concrete. These types of blocks are called Insulated Concrete Forms (ICFs). Figure 1-7b shows remnant block pieces after cutting.

Insulated Concrete Forms

In the Herbe design the first two floors are framed using the ICF (Styrofoam) blocks; the third floor is built with wood. (Like most chateaux, Herbe has a mansard roof: a steeply tilted wall that provides the top floor of living space or a "super attic.") The block provides insulation as well as the interior and exterior wall surface, and the poured concrete columns provide structural integrity. The manufacturer claims the blocks are cost effective, and are more ecological than wood because they are made out of recycled packaging materials. My blocks are made from a blend of 85% recycled Styrofoam and 15% concrete. When you hold a piece of this material in your hand, it's much heavier than ordinary Styrofoam. The blocks can be worked with hand tools, and are a substitute for the large sandstone or limestone blocks used in antiquity. Chapter 4 gives more details on the novel materials used and more information on building with ICF blocks.

The insulation benefits of these blocks are significant — according to the vendors, the blocks have low heat conductance and a high insulation rating (~R25). The benefits go beyond just insulation, however. Both the concrete cells and steel reinforcement have a high mass. The block walls don't change temperature very rapidly. This high "thermal mass" tends to smooth out temperature changes, causing the building to "lag" — cooling slowly at night and warming slowly by day. This reduces your heating and cooling costs.

Since a chateau needs to have a more massive structural look, and heating and cooling are important, I chose to use 10"-thick ICF blocks for my exterior walls.

Figure 1-8a: Herbe phase 2 garage end and front view

Figure 1-8b: Herbe phase 2 garage end and rear view

Bottom-Up Issues

The goals of building an expandable house and using Styrofoam blocks turned out to be somewhat contradictory, since the blocks have limitations that affect both the architecture and the construction sequence. For example, the size of the blocks affected the dimensions of the building as will be explained in Chapter 2. But perhaps most significantly, the choice of building material eliminated the option of building up from a one story structure.

Architects discourage adding concrete sections vertically; the additions on top may not form a solid connection with the underlying structure, making the building unsafe in an earthquake. Therefore, as a consequence of using Styrofoam and concrete, the Herbe house has been built in adjacent left/right sections rather than in horizontal layers (phase 1 is option 4 in Table 1). Figure 1-8 shows the phase 2 addition; ICF blocks are attached to the left side of the first-phase building. More details on these blocks are given in Chapter 4, and their effect on Herbe's architecture is discussed in Chapter 2.

Note in these photos that the second-phase, a 3,000 sq. ft. left wing and tower, are being added to the phase 1 building about 2 years after the completion and occupancy of the first phase, a two-bedroom, 2 ½-bath house. As can be seen in the photo, there are no windows on the left-end upper floors of the phase 1 building, since that original exterior wall becomes an interior wall in phase 2. However, underneath the stucco exterior, and not visible in the photograph, are doorframes on the second and third floors that will interconnect the building's sections. In Figure 1-8a, the external foyer door on the first floor becomes the door to the study added in phase 2. On the other hand, the small powder room window adjacent to the foyer door is eliminated when the phase 2 addition is implemented. These low-level interfacing details need to be set in the early plan to allow for the additional construction.

The phase 1 building's roofline is not typical of the end of a chateau, and look more like a barn. This end becomes hidden when the adjacent phase is completed, as will be shown later. However, this roof design is easy to extend across the adjacent wing with the identical cross section. Often the roofline of a building severely limits expansion; in this case it facilitates it.

Lessons Learned: Providing for expansion sometimes looks strange.

The phase 1 garden room protruding to the rear has a deck above and is described in more detail in Chapter 2. There is no garage in the phase 1 building; this is added on the end of the phase 2 building shown in Figure 1-8a — note the two garage door spaces.

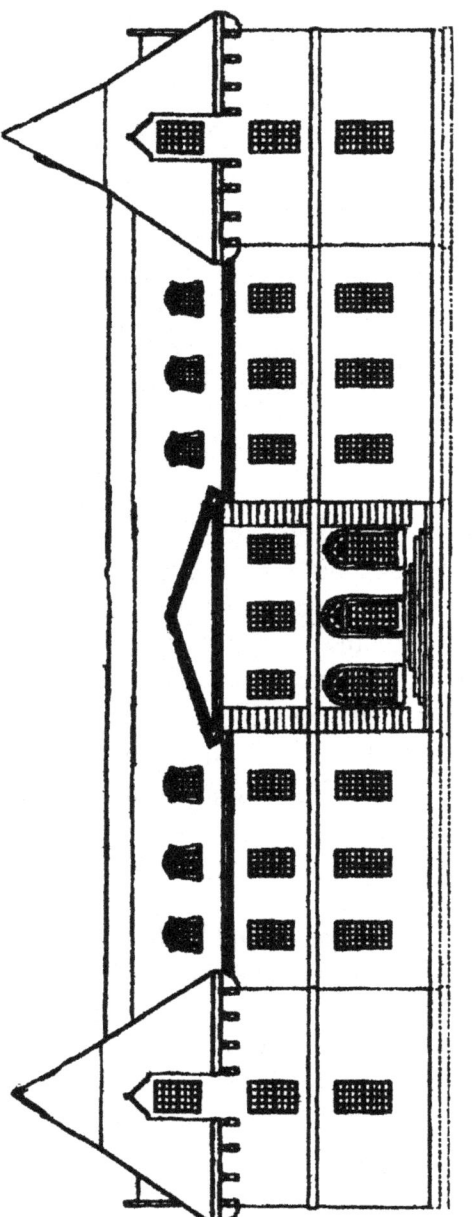

Figure 2-1a: Chateau Herbe front elevation

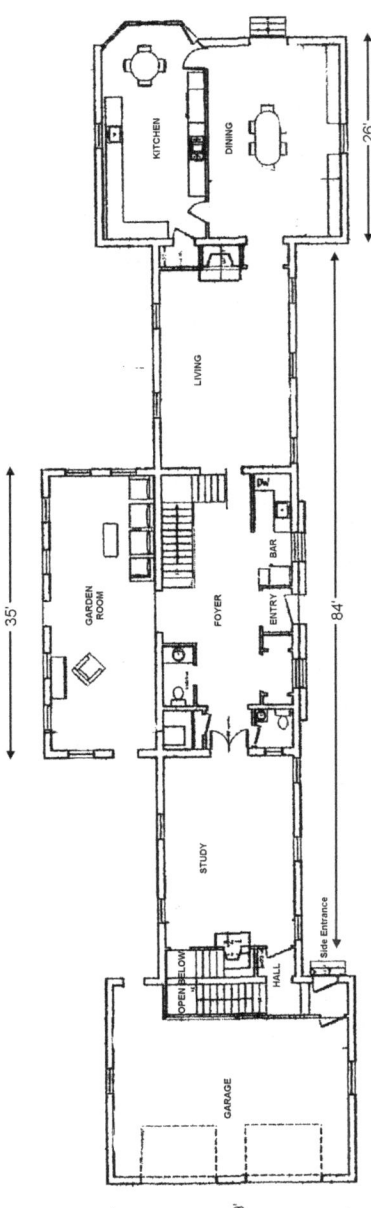

Figure 2-1b: Chateau Herbe 1st floor plan

Chapter 2
The Design

This chapter describes the architectural design of my Chateau Herbe. Some of the issues and solutions that emerged in the design process are explained for the benefit of the novice designer. While not all of the final details of a multi-phased project need to be set at the beginning, the design must clearly define how the first construction phase integrates with subsequent stages. For this reason, the design was developed in a top-down manner starting with the overall look and shape of the structure. Chapter 5 reports the successes and problems of the building integration in multiple phases, and on some of the interior design issues. On the other hand, the building's size was chosen in a bottom-up manner and is described to give the reader some insight into choosing some critical dimensions.

Inspired by a Norman chateau built in 1630, I proposed the design for Chateau Herbe as a two-tower project, with which design consultants in Oregon agreed. Neoclassic designs require symmetry; therefore Herbe's windows and towers are symmetric, as shown in the front elevation in Figure 2-1a, and in the ground-level floor plan in Figure 2-1b. The 84'-long center includes a central foyer with a garden room to the rear, a living room in the right wing and a study in the left wing. The two symmetric 26'-long towers hold the kitchen and dining room (right) and the two-car garage (left). The driveway and garage doors are concealed on the left end, since a historic chateau wouldn't have had a car garage. An extra 16' appendage (nook) was added to the far right in phase 4, as described in chapter 5.

By modern standards, this isn't an ideal layout. A square shape is more practical, and the garage should be closer to the kitchen. However, since fidelity to 17th-century architecture was a higher priority than 21st-century tastes, the layout retains the long, shallow footprint of the original chateau. In classic chateaux there are often no corridors; the rooms simply abut, and an open passageway ("cartoid") extends in a straight line through the heart of the chateau, allowing a continuous view through the length of the building. Following this tradition, Herbe has no hallway; from the end of the study you can see through the foyer, the living room and the dining room. Also following classic style, the doorways in this passage are centered in their walls. From the foyer, double pocket doors lead to the study, and an under-the-stairway "tunnel" leads to the living room and the right tower.

A key decision is the ceiling height in each of the building's levels. I chose 10' for all floors — a decision I've regretted multiple times. Generally the ground level of a chateau should have a more impressive height, and the upstairs bedrooms could have been 9' tall. I describe in this chapter some small workarounds to gain a few extra inches.

Several stairways lead to the second and third floors, with the principal staircase located on the right-hand side of the foyer, going up to the right. All of the bedrooms are upstairs. Because staircase design is an important design element, the configuration of the steps is explained in great detail at the end of this chapter, as well as how the staircase size influenced the design of the foyer.

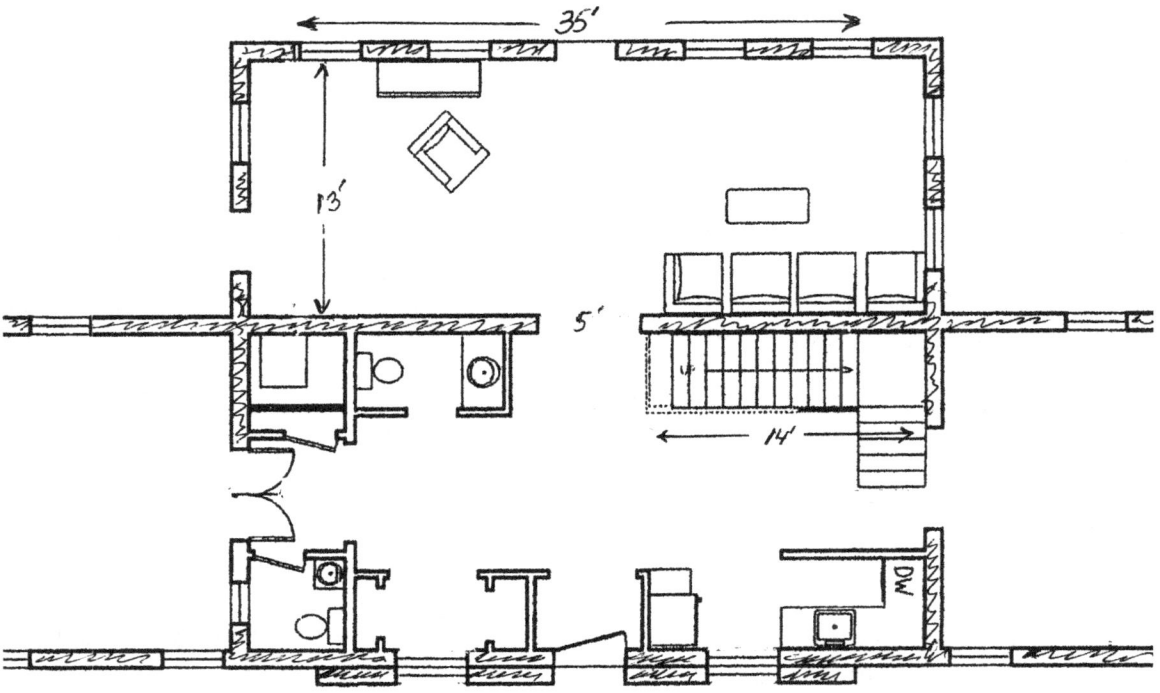

Figure 2-2a: Floor plan for center section 1st floor

Figure 2-2b: View of front door from foyer

Design Details

The overall dimensions of my Chateau Herbe are different from those of the Norman chateau. My first choice for Herbe's width was the Norman chateau's 16', but constraints imposed by the building materials immediately forced me to revise this. Since it was better to have a concrete cell at each corner, and since there's 15" between cells, I had two reasonable choices for the width: 15'5" or 16'8", and reduced the target 16' to the final width of 15'5". Block details are in Chapter 4.

Lessons Learned: Select building materials as part of the architecture.

Herbe's tower, wings, and central section mimic the proportions of the original chateau, but my initial 136' length is about 80% of the original chateau's size. This length was the result of a bottom-up calculation. The Herbe building length is the sum of the room lengths (plus the stairwells). I didn't know the room sizes in the Norman chateau, and since I was choosing my own unique floor plan the room sizes were a matter of personal taste.

Room Length
- 23' living room/study
- 23' bedroom (with bathroom and closet)
- 26' garage, kitchen/dining - tower
- 33' foyer and garden room

I prefer a smaller foyer; however, the 33' foyer length is set by the 14' length of the staircase, which in turn depends upon the ceiling height. These details were chosen and incorporated into the floor plan from the beginning. Additionally, the fixed symmetric window placements affect the room size — a wall separating two rooms can't be in the middle of a window. On the other hand, the two 26' long end towers weren't specified until the second and fourth design phase, and the 16' nook appendage was added in phase 4.

The first-phase design focused on the center section details, shown in Figure 2-2a. The foyer is in the center, the garden room to the rear; the interfaces are defined for the left and right wings (built in later phases). The open passage to the garden room is directly at the rear of the foyer, centered left to right. The foyer is in a pivotal position, offering access to the key rooms, and for large parties guests circulate among these principal rooms.

Entry and Foyer: Figure 2-2b shows an early construction photograph looking out through the arched entry from the foyer. It also shows the adjacent front foyer's arched window, and the future location of the guest closet shown in the floor plan to the left of the entry. There are two powder rooms (men, ladies), and a bar off of the foyer. In the first phase the guest closet and extra powder room were delayed to provide more living space-- for a desk and couch. The wet bar is expanded and is the temporary kitchen during phase 1.

Lessons Learned: Postpone some interior walls till needed.

Figure 2-3a: Norman chateau rear center view

Figure 2-3b: Chateau Herbe rear center view

Study and Living Room: The 23'x15'5" study and living room are placed symmetrically around the foyer and have identical window placements — a requirement in neoclassic designs. Each has a fireplace. The study is finished with wood paneling and has a beamed ceiling, described in detail in Chapter 5 and shown in Figure 5-17b. The entrance to each room is 5' wide, centered in both the end wall and the foyer's wall. A pair of pocket doors defines the entries to the study and the living room. Both the study and living room are reached by passing through an arched tunnel about 5' long. Although this is slightly excessive, it provides space for the HVAC, powder room, and stairway. Figure 5-14 shows the living room finishing.

Garden Room: While the Norman chateau has no separate garden room, Herbe's design incorporates one in order to enhance the outdoor feeling of the house and to take advantage of the views of Mount Ashland. The garden room's eight windows allow considerable sunlight to enter because of the room's southern exposure (described in Chapter 3). The garden room extends the footprint of Herbe's center section an additional 13' to the rear, compared to the two adjacent wings. As a consequence, as seen in the photographs in Figure 2-3, the rear elevations of Herbe (below) and the original chateau are quite different. In phase 1 the garden room serves as both the living and dining room; see Figure 6-6a.

Second Floor Deck: Above Herbe's garden room, a second floor deck (Figure 2-3b) provides an outdoor exposure for the upstairs den via a pair of French doors. In phase 1, this room is the master bedroom. The deck is designed so rainwater runs to its far corners and out decorative scuppers and gargoyles on the rear balustrade as seen in Figure 6-3b. See Figure 1-8b for the side profile of the deck.

Back Porch: Maurine, my wife, suggested adding a back porch at the rear of the garden room, as a pleasant spot for guests to congregate. Herbe's concrete porch is elevated above the ground, level with the garden room and main foyer. Its centered steps lead to the lawn. The handrail, visible in the picture in Figure 2-3b, is required by local building codes, and was not intended in my original design.

Exterior Trim: Herbe's exterior features a little more trim than that of the Norman chateau, as shown in Figure 2-3b. The trim in the front and the rear is made of flat-stock Styrofoam, explained in Chapter 4; it is easily cut with hand tools (Figure 6-4a) to fashion window surrounds and exterior sills. Since most surrounds on classic buildings are built from cut blocks of stone, the flat stock was cut into blocks and glued together to emulate this style.

View to Rear: From the front door of the Norman chateau, you can see directly through to the rear garden, as shown in Figure 2-4a. This was a key requirement of the design that can be seen in Figure 2-4b. Accordingly, the central stairway needed to fit entirely on one side of the foyer to meet this requirement as will be described later in detail.

Figure 2-4a: Norman chateau front center view

Figure 2-4b: Chateau Herbe front center view

Foyer Design Issues

Foyer Width

The Herbe foyer is centered and provides access to the adjacent study (phase 2 left), living room (phase 3 right) and garden room, as shown in the floor plan in Figure 2-2a. In the chateau in Normandy, the foyer is one foot deeper than the adjacent wing; this 12" forward projection, including the decorative quoins, is both classic and attractive, as shown in Figure 2-4a. In this photo, taken in our 1997 trip, my wife, Maurine, is holding a measuring stick and, as she is standing, is also being used as a measuring stick herself.

However, duplicating this wider foyer would require Herbe's foundation to have two expensive jogs, and the trivial increase in floor space did not justify the added cost. To simplify the foundation design, Herbe's front wall is in line with the adjoining wings (living room and study). As a compromise, and to create a look similar to the Normandy façade, the fascia blocks on the front center section were doubled to project the wall forward by 10", as shown in Figure 2-2a (floor plan), near the entry and the bar, rather than making the room itself larger.

This double-block, 20"-thick front wall of Herbe is reminiscent of the cut stone blocks used in many of the French chateaux, and the weightiness of the building is apparent as you approach (see the photo Figure 2-4b). This "false" front is a good compromise between form and function, and provides extra insulation. Inside the foyer, the windowsills in this double wall are quite deep as well. Note also that the Herbe front door is centered left and right for symmetry.

Lessons Learned: Form and function often conflict, requiring tradeoffs.

Foyer Height

While the ceilings in most modern homes are 8' high, an elegant chateau's might be much higher — 12'-16'. The height of the Norman chateau's ceilings is not published, but in magazine photos it appeared to be about 10'. Therefore, I determined, Herbe's ceilings would be 10' high. This turned out to be something of a miscalculation, and I now think the Norman chateau's first-floor ceilings are closer to 11'. My new design failed to account for the added height of trim and moldings — see below. Once this height was chosen it was pretty difficult to change any of the other room heights, but I did pick up a few extra inches, as described later, in the study and the living room ceilings.

Here is the math: the side doors are 78" tall x 60" wide, with a transom window 4" above them, placing the 30"-radius arch top at 112". So a 10' (120") ceiling height seems to provide 8" of clearance above the transom. However, a typical door surround trim is 5" wide, and a ceiling crown molding adds 5"; hence, the ceiling is 2" too short for these trimmings!

Lessons Learned: Include window surrounds and moldings in calculations.

Figure 2-5a: View of foyer stairwell and kitchen

Figure 2-5b: View at bottom of stairway

Foyer Length

As previously discussed, the foyer's width is 15'5", but its 33' length is determined by two important factors:

- The foyer must be symmetric around the front door
- The stairway shouldn't block the view out the back

Since it's desirable to have an unobstructed view out to the back yard through the rear of the foyer, the stairway needs to fit entirely on the foyer's right side, as in Figure 2-5a. The stairway length was the determining factor for the foyer's length. These dimensions are so tight that the bottom step just barely clears the garden room doorway, see Figure 2-5b, and the door surround molding may not fit. Since the stairs and landing require a total run of 14', the foyer's 33' interior length is determined as follows:

5'	- centered passageway to garden room (Figure 2-2a)
14'	- length of stairwell to the right of the passageway
<u>14'</u>	- length of rear left wall - for symmetry
33'	- total foyer length

Design for Expansion

The photo in figure 2-5a shows an end side wall of the foyer during phase 1 construction (the interim kitchen is located in this end; see 5-3b also). The temporary exterior window was stick framed and will be an arched doorway to the living room in the future. To simplify changeover later, no electrical wires were run across this future doorway.

Lessons Learned:
- Include door moldings when calculating stairway clearance.
- Don't run wiring or plumbing through future doorways.

One drawback of this design is that in phase 1 the side of the stairwell and the reduced ceiling height are plainly visible, as shown in the photo Figure 2-5a. In successive phases a barrel ceiling and an arched passageway will hide the stairwell above the arched window. In theory, a wall could be used now to shield this area and conceal the stairwell, but since the interim kitchen is located in this end of the foyer, it's not practical to do so. This is a classic example of one tradeoff with incremental construction: room arrangements that are less than ideal. Chapter 5 gives some of the interim kitchen details.

Another less than pleasing feature of the phase 1 building is that the view of the end of the building looks a lot like a barn, Figure 1-8, and not much like a chateau. Normally there would be a sloped roofline on the end, or a mansard finish. The abrupt end makes it very easy to extend the phase 1 building roof, but it isn't very pretty.

Lessons Learned: Interim results are often not optimum.

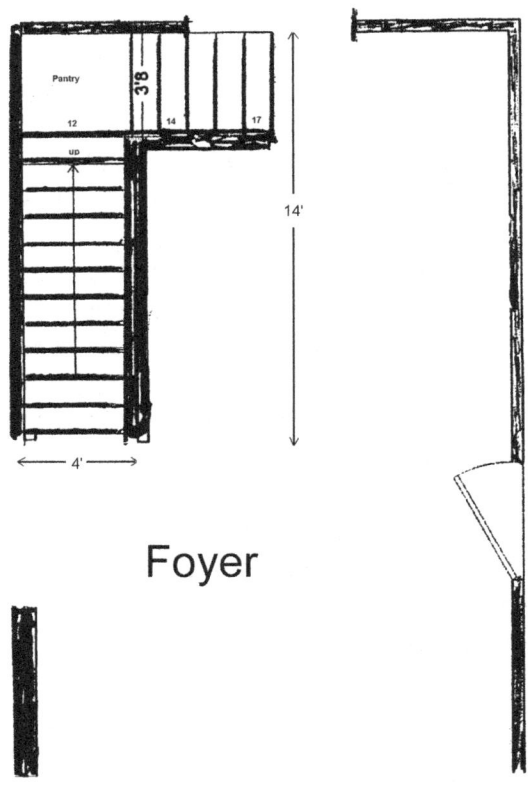

Figure 2-6a: Foyer L-stairway plan

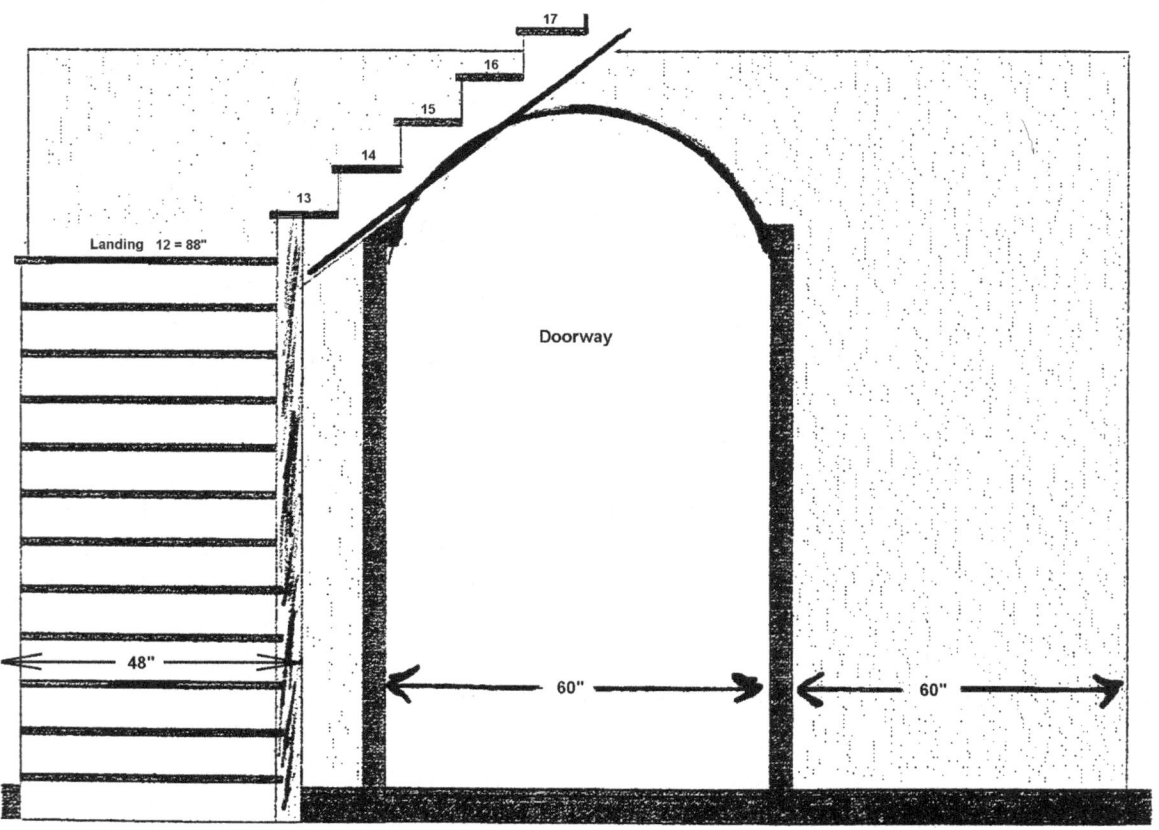

Figure 2-6b: Stairwell plan and elevation

Staircase Design Choices

Staircases can be simply functional (4' wide) or more extravagant (5'-8' wide), allowing two people to stand side by side and make a grand entrance. Most chateaux are multi-story, with very grand, prominent stairwells. The design of the stairwell is one of the first important decisions to be made in a multi-story structure. I chose a more functional and modest 42"-wide, 17-step staircase with wrought-iron trim.

Part of a floor plan design is choosing the location, orientation, and general configuration of the stairway. One factor in choosing the staircase shape is the amount of floor space consumed by the stairs — is it more desirable to use some of the room's width, or its length? Since each stair tread is about 11" deep, the 17 stairs require 187", about 16 linear feet. Additionally, space needs to be allocated for a 4' landing at the top and bottom of the stairway (as explained below), for a total of at least 24 linear feet; an intermediate landing requires additional space. A single 24'-long stairway won't fit the 15.5' front-to-back depth of the Herbe foyer; even if it could fit, a single run of stairs is hazardous because there's nothing to break the fall if someone should tumble down the steps. For this reason, staircases are usually split into multiple sections, typically into an L or a U.

L-Shaped Stairway

Herbe's ground floor stairway is an L, as shown in Figure 2-5a. The long leg, 11 stairs, runs along the back wall of the foyer to a middle landing, from which the short leg of five stairs runs along the sidewall, back to front. This long leg requires only 4' of the foyer's width, as shown in Figure 2-6a, but its 14' length is crucial at the design stage, as mentioned earlier, for determining the foyer's overall length.

Stairway Tunnel

This stairway L in the foyer creates a tunnel, shown in Figure 2-6b, underneath the stairway to access the adjacent living room; this technique is used in many classic chateaux. The stairs must be high enough to allow at least a 78"-tall doorway underneath. The stair support stringer requires approximately 10" or more. This means that the stair tread must be at a height of at least 88" (78" + 10") from the floor over the doorway. With 7.3" stair risers, the first stair step that's high enough to allow for a doorway is #12. (7.3"x 12 = 88"). So the location of the stairwell determines where a passageway to an adjacent room can be placed. Herbe's L configuration provides a centered passageway into the living room. Also note that Herbe's 10' ceiling calls for a taller-than-normal doorway. Accordingly, the living-room doorway (a window in phase 1) starts under tread #14. Since there's even more headroom at the center of the doorway, an arched passageway is possible. The arch clearance grows, and the center of the arch is under tread #17; see Figure 2-6b for the archway clearance under the stairway and the photo in Figure 2-5a, and also Figure 5-3. Recall that in later phases there will be an arched passageway concealing steps #13-#17. I later realized if the ground floor had a higher ceiling, the first leg of my stairwell would have provided an adequate tunnel to the adjacent room without lengthening the foyer.

Lessons Learned: A stairway tunnel needs 78+" of height.

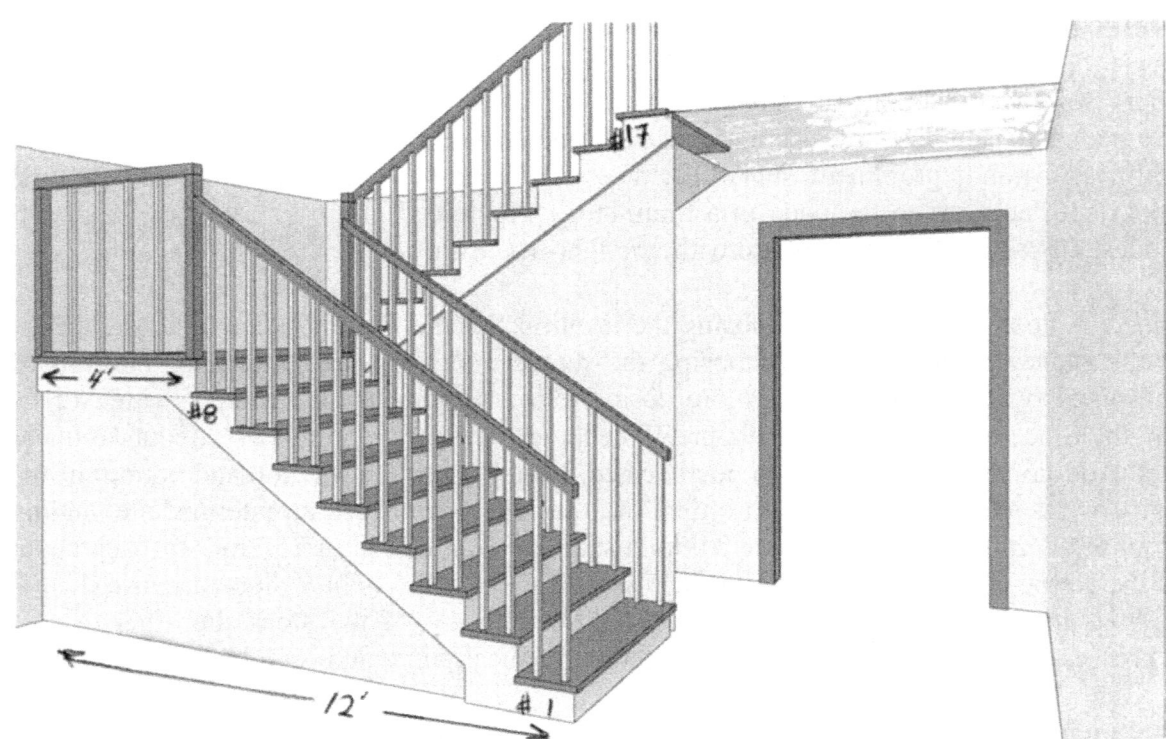

Figure 2-7a: U-stairwell perspective drawing

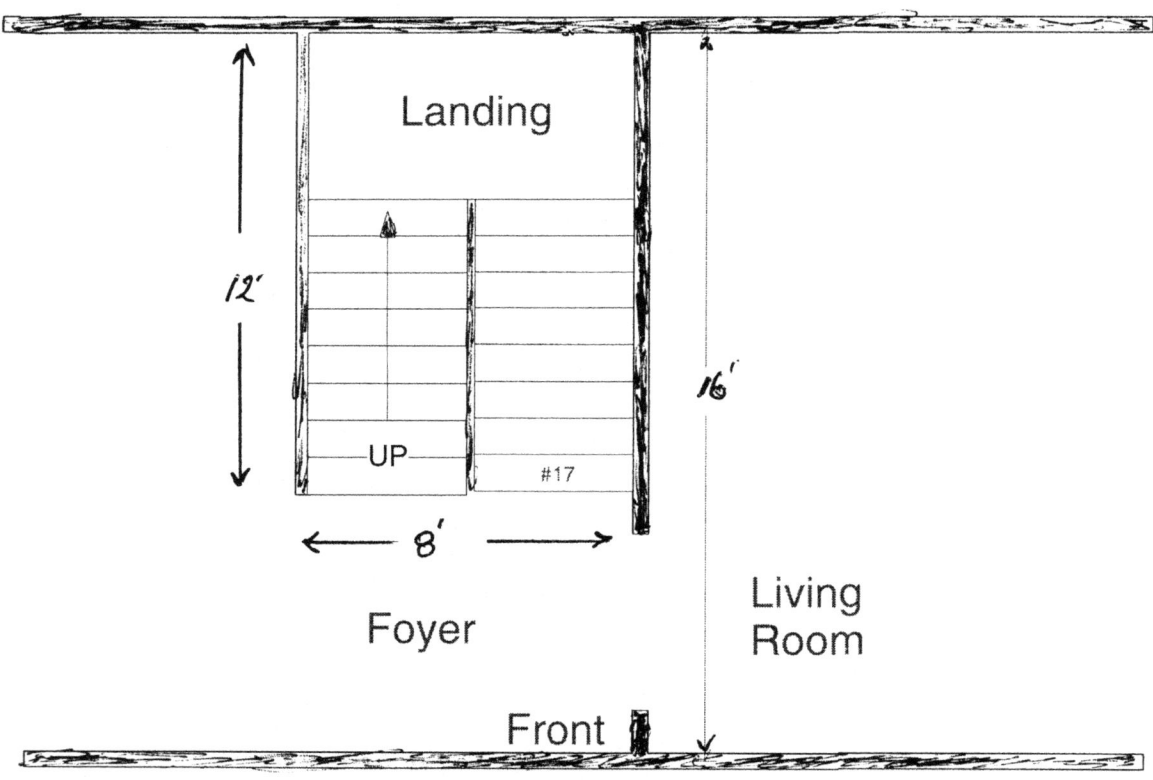

Figure 2-7b: U-stairwell floor plan

U-Shaped Stairway

Herbe's second floor staircase is a more conventional U-shaped stairway, similar to that shown in Figure 2-7a; the base of the stairs is located on the left side of the U. The staircase occupies about 8' of room length (4' x 2) and about 12' of room width, but the 4' landing brings the total width to 16'. (Sometimes a closet can be placed under the high part of the stairwell.) The total linear length of the stairwell is 32' (16' x 2), commonly split into two equal 16' sections:

4'	bottom landing	4'	middle landing
8'	steps	8'	steps
4'	middle landing	4'	top landing
16'	total	16'	total

This 16' is a close match to the Herbe building width. However, the U-shaped staircase provides a 4' wide passageway in front of the stairwell. Because symmetry is important in neoclassic design, I wanted the doorway to be centered in the living room wall, as shown in Figure 2-6b. This made a U-shaped stairwell a poor choice in the foyer (as shown in Figure 2-7b), as the door to the living room would not be centered. However, since the bedroom doors on the second and third floor are near the front of the house, the U-shaped stairwell worked out fine for the upper floors as shown in the floor plan in Figure 2-8.

Stair Math

The calculations presented here reflect the design process for my particular stairway configuration, but may also interest a new designer. Stairwell engineering has some basic requirements: the stairway must reach from the first to the second floor with a continuous set of steps and landings, all of the same height. Stairway design is constrained by the height to be climbed and the horizontal distance available. Most construction books give guidelines for safe staircase treads and risers, but check local building codes. Typically, stair risers are 6.5" to 7.5" tall, and stair treads are 10" to 12" deep.

As previously noted, the foyer's ceiling height is 120" (10'). Allowing an additional 12" for the thickness of the joists separating the first and second floors, the second floor is 132" (120" + 12") above the ground floor. We need an integral number of identical risers. Several choices are available:

       17 risers = 132"/17 = 7.764"/riser
       18 risers = 132"/18 = 7.333"/riser → this is the chosen value
       19 risers = 132"/19 = 6.947"/riser

A lesser riser height is more elegant, but requires more steps and consequently occupies more floor space. I compromised in the case of my Herbe design, and chose 18 risers to reach the second floor, requiring 17 stair treads to the landing above, as shown in the Figures 2-7. The first eight stair treads occupy (8 x 11") or about 7 ½'; adding a 4' landing brings the total near 12', as indicated in Figures 2-7, and leaves about 4' for the lower landing also. Figure 2-6b also shows the 17 stair treads needed for the L-shaped first-to-second floor stairway.

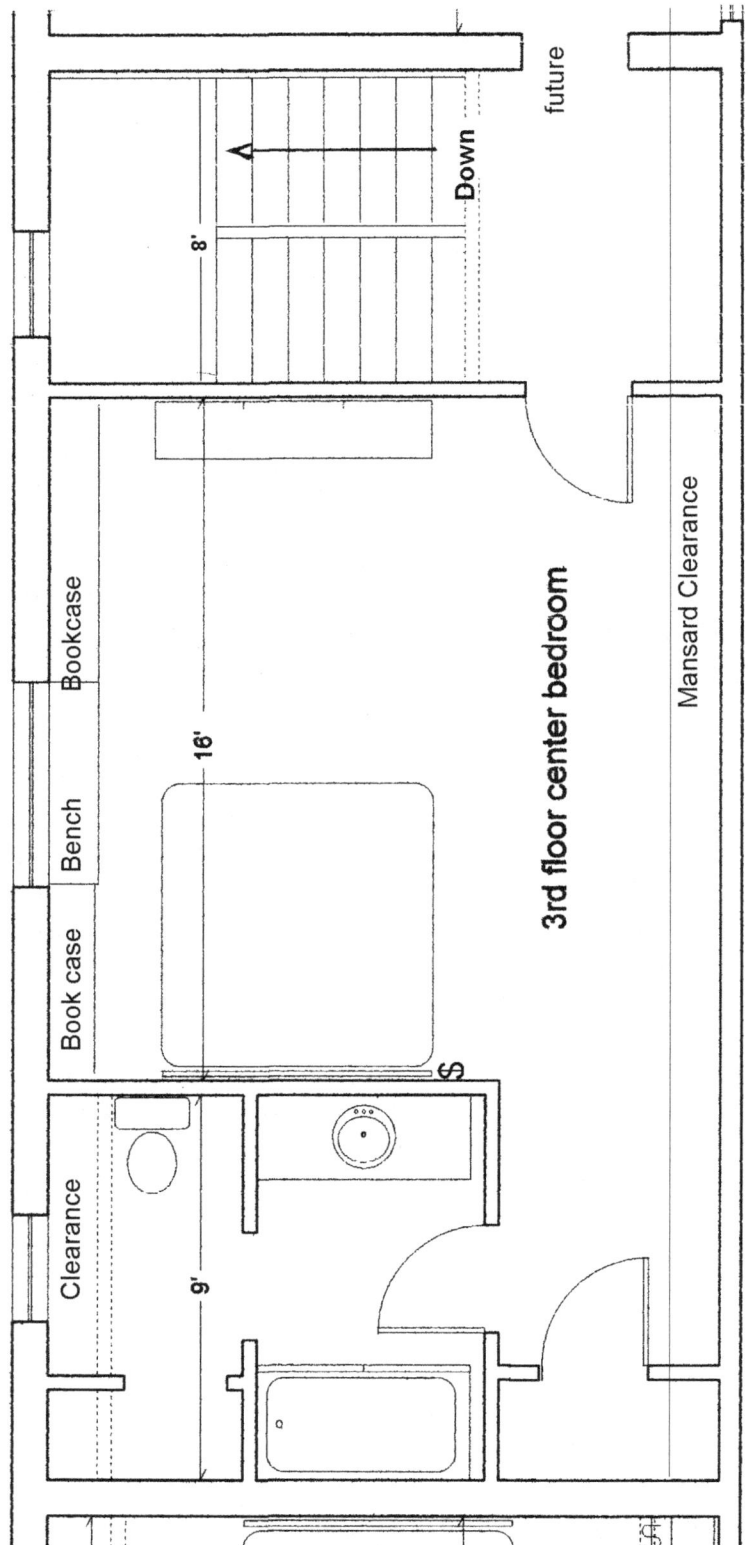

Figure 2-8: Third floor bedroom floor plan

Upper Floor Room Layouts

As described earlier, the foyer is 33' long (Figure 2-2a) and sets the phase 1 building's size. Using an 8'-wide stairway leaves 25' for the upstairs room length (33' - 8' stairwell). Most of Herbe's bedrooms are ~16' square, and each has its own private bathroom, so the 25' is split between a 16' bedroom and 9' bathroom and closet, as shown in the third-floor layout in Figure 2-8. The placement and orientation of the stairway in the foyer also dictate the location of the bedroom entry door — towards the front of the building. Another (future) door is also framed to access subsequent phase 3 bedrooms. The mansard style roof limits the headroom within 18" of the outer walls of this third story bedroom; see Figure 5-18a. Hence the doorways are more inboard, the toilet is set further in, and a window bench and bookcase are at the rear wall of this bedroom as shown in the diagram in Figure 2-8.

Window placements are part of a room's design, and in Herbe's case must accommodate, the symmetric window locations determined by the external architecture. Most window locations follow those of the original chateau; window sizes are scaled to ~80%. In Herbe's phase 1 third-floor bedroom, Figure 2-8, there are no front windows because of the classic decorative pediment shown in Figure 1-3a. The large rear center window, Figure 2-3b and Figure 4-9b, falls off-center in the bedroom's rear wall. These window placements and their views influence the future furniture layout, and subsequent user traffic patterns. I placed the light switch based on what I assumed would be the position of the bed. In fact we've tried three different locations for the bed, but the light switch location is fixed. Nevertheless, in designing a room, consider where you will most likely place the furniture.

Bedroom Layout
Among the desirable aesthetic goals for bedroom design:

- Exterior rear view is visible from the bed
- The bed headboard is visible from the bedroom entrance
- A light switch is 24" off the floor adjacent to the bed
- The dresser is 5' across from the bed
- The bathroom vanity is 5' long
- The toilet room is separate from the rest of the bathroom
- The closet is not visible from the bedroom entrance
- The closet is a sound buffer for the bathroom

The design shown in Figure 2-8 does not meet all these goals. Other options include reversing the placement of the dresser and bed, or rearranging the bathroom. I used my home PC's computer drafting system to produce diagrams such as Figure 2-8 to explore alternate layouts and visualize the 3-D relationships within the rooms. I faxed these draft floor plans to my designers in Oregon. They then created the actual plans, considering the structural requirements, building codes, and materials, and faxed me the revised plans.

Note: an architect's trick makes the building appear taller — windows on each floor are shorter than the windows below. For example, the window heights in the wing are:
First floor 78"; second floor 60"; dormers 42", as shown in Figure 2-1a.

ASHLAND QUADRANGLE
OREGON—JACKSON CO.
7.5 MINUTE SERIES (TOPOGRAPHIC)

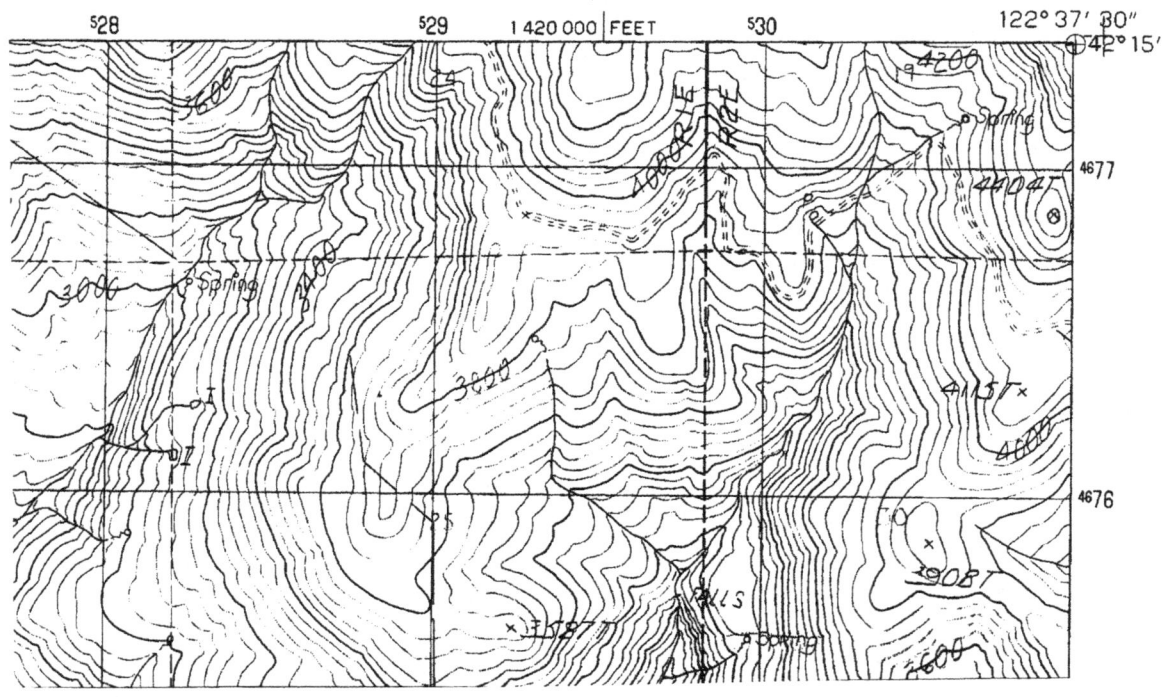

Figure 3-1a: Sample topographic map

Figure 3-1b: Ashland home site view

Chapter 3
Land and Site Plan

Ancient fortified castles in Europe often formed the basis for a town that grew along the castle wall. On the other hand, most grand manor houses and "newer" chateaux are set on large, isolated parcels, surrounded with considerable open landscaping. The Norman chateau sits by itself except for a nearby caretaker house; see Figure 1-1a.

Placing a chateau in a modern setting presents some difficulties. While many find the style itself attractive, a large, opulent home that is out of scale for the surroundings or doesn't fit the neighborhood character is unlikely to be popular. For the benefit of the neighbors and for the owners' privacy, it's desirable to isolate a new building from nearby dwellings.

In defining our search for Herbe's site, we decided that we wanted a parcel of land close to the town of Ashland, but isolated from neighbors. Since this ruled out most city lots, we looked for acreage outside the city limits, and found that rural properties require greater infrastructure development and more site planning than their urban counterparts. Furthermore, there can be unexpected legal restrictions and other pitfalls. While each site has unique issues, my experiences in developing my particular site may be useful to other would-be builders.

Site Selection

Rural land is often reviewed on maps such as Figure 3-1a; they give the outlines of the terrain using topographic contour lines that allow you to determine how the terrain lies, and where the flat building sites are. We found a 25-acre agricultural parcel in Jackson County, Oregon, just outside the Ashland city limits, listed for sale through a real estate broker. Its advantages were a private location, mostly flat terrain, and creek side boundary. Its disadvantages were a flood plain (the creek flooded often), highway noise (Highway 5 was adjacent to the property), and poor soils (the heavy clay soil tended to hold water and swell when wet, which would cause problems with the building's foundation and the septic system). Although it wasn't an ideal site, I purchased this parcel, Figure 3-1b.

Buying undeveloped land differs somewhat from buying residential property. One crucial issue: generally banks don't lend money on bare land. Fortunately, my broker arranged seller financing for the land purchase, so monthly payments of principal and interest go to the seller instead of to a bank. In 1995, when I bought the property, land cost between $10k and $40k/acre, depending upon location, topology, soils, and improvements. We'll see later in this chapter the costs of adding utilities to this lot. By contrast, a finished quarter-acre city lot with building permit and utilities cost around $50k, depending on location.

Lessons Learned:
- Financing undeveloped land differs from financing developed property; if the seller has clear title, he can carry the loan.
- Undeveloped land involves more risks.

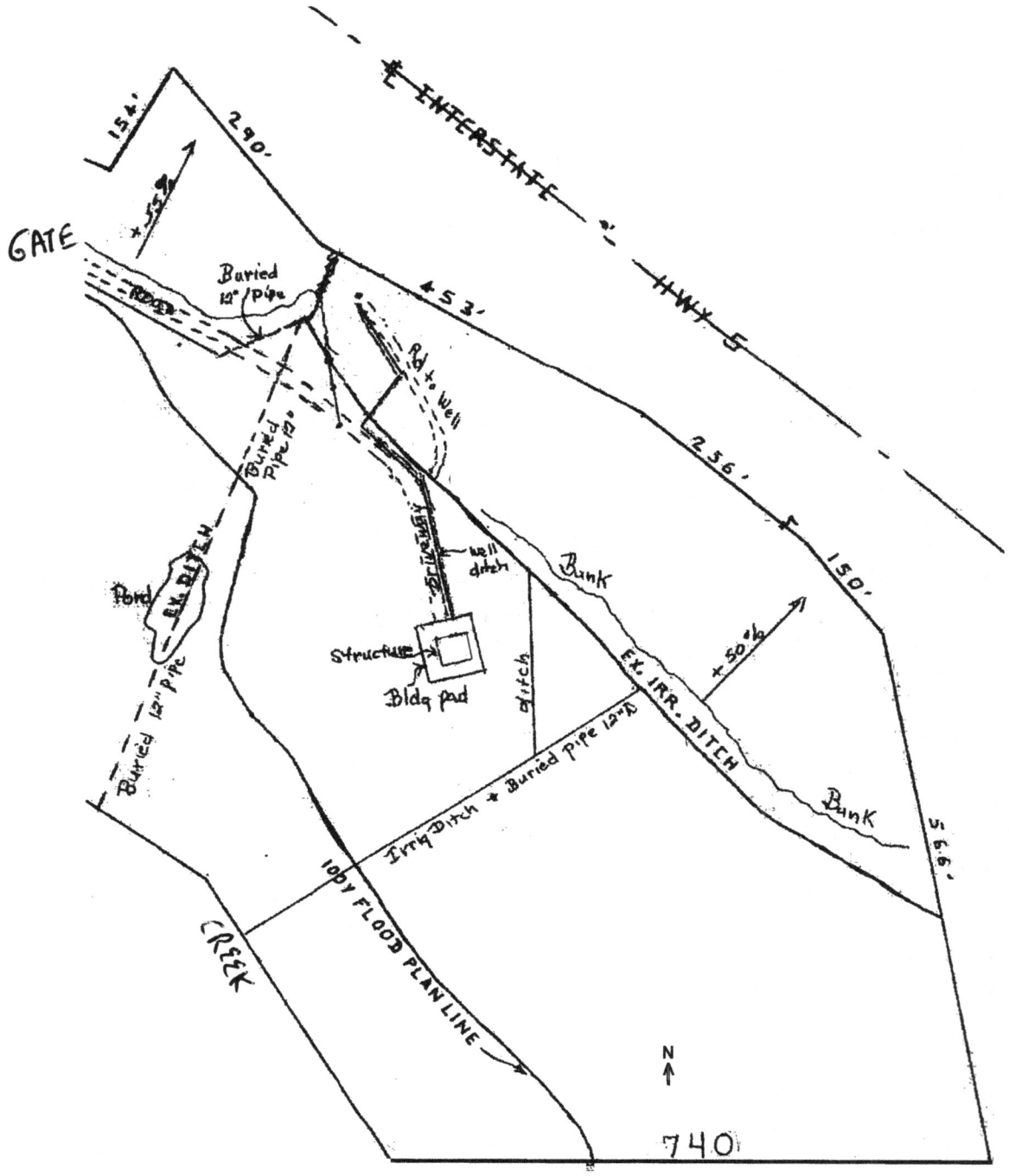

Figure 3-2: Draft site plan

Zoning and Regulatory Issues

Building permits and land uses are more varied outside the city limits than inside them, and a land parcel's value varies considerably according to its location and zoning. This particular parcel was county land, zoned agricultural — which required special approval to build a house.

A benefit of agricultural zoning for farmers (and land speculators) is that the county's property taxes are reduced while the land is used for agriculture. The downside is that as soon as you improve the property or use it for something other than agriculture, you may lose the lower tax rate, and you're assessed at the higher rate going forward (and also retroactively in many cases).

More issues arose after I commissioned a local land developer to apply to the county planning department for a building permit on my behalf. The county required soil analysis and independent recommendations, but after eight weeks gave permission to build a single home — with significant restrictions. I was not able to freely choose the location of the house on the property; instead, the county planner chose the home site using data we'd submitted about the lot, along with existing standards. As a result, the home site is 1,200' from the street and the gate, and 450' from the adjacent creek, and outside of the 100-year flood plain line. Figure 3-2 shows the site plan, with the location for the building pad, the setbacks from the neighboring properties, the driveways and the utilities.

In addition, as conditions for the permit, the county required a number of covenants — including one mandating that, despite the 25-acre size of the parcel and the fence that surrounded it, dogs could not be off leash on any part of the property. These covenants are binding on all future owners of the property. Also this lot, like many agricultural parcels smaller than 40 acres, cannot be further subdivided and sold piecemeal. And, as noted above, I was charged three years' penalty tax as part of the permit process.

Lessons Learned:
- Investigate the permitted uses and the associated development risks.
- Investigate the property tax implications for changing land use.

Infrastructure

The county planning department wouldn't issue a building permit unless water and sewage treatment were available. Within the city limit, these services are readily available. However, since this parcel was outside Ashland's boundary, it didn't have access to these services, which meant I needed a septic system and a well; electricity was already available on all sides, on the neighboring properties. The riskiest installations are the water and septic systems, since both require a survey and search; therefore, it's sensible to do these more speculative tasks first. While it would have been convenient to have power for testing the well pump, electricity wasn't installed until after the water and septic were in place.

Lessons Learned:
- Both water and septic systems require investigations and permits.
- Do the work with the most risk first.

Figure 3-3a: Water wellhead

Figure 3-3b: View of creek side boundary

Costs

Installing these systems is an expense, but once they're installed they add significantly to the property's value. In 1998, when I had the work done, the utility installation costs were:

Electricity ($100/foot x 1,200')	$12k
Septic (survey, permits, system)	$12k
Water well (survey, drilling, pump)	$12k
	$36k

Notice that utilities cost almost $40,000; for a 20-acre parcel, this adds about $2k/acre.

Water Well

Based upon the land's topology, a local geologist chose a well site at a fault, where water is likely to be closer to the surface. The driller found water beneath solid rock at a depth of 70', but we continued drilling in hopes of finding a deeper and perhaps better water source. However, at 120' we hadn't found a second source, so we stopped drilling. (The project is billed per foot drilled, with the owner taking the financial risk.)

As shown in Figure 3-3a, a steel casing was set into the drilled hole, and a pump test was run using a portable pump, since electricity wasn't yet available. The test indicated a suitable flow rate (10 gallons/minute) for domestic usage. I postponed water quality testing for a few months, since it would cost several hundred dollars. (These tests eventually showed a trace amount of bacteria until the well was flushed and chlorinated, after which the water passed all tests.) After the electrical system was in place, we installed a submersible pump that sent water to a pressure holding tank located in the house. After four years of usage I added a 2,000-gallon aboveground water tank adjacent to the well. I believe this lowers the burden of the in-ground pump, and provides enough water to source an in-house fire suppression system. We also added a couple of water softeners after determining that the hard water was detrimental to the plumbing system and fixtures. We have four electric water heaters in total; they were installed as each building section was added.

Lessons Learned:
- Size water pipes for the eventual large house and multiple water heaters.

Irrigation

An important concern on agricultural land is the availability of water for crop irrigation. Since the well doesn't provide enough water for landscaping, another system brings water from Bear Creek. Figure 3-3b shows this creek side property boundary that is an asset for both the irrigation water and the views. An old pump house has been used continuously for crop irrigation, and a water lawyer determined my legal portion of the creek's water. After the electrical system was in place, we installed a new electric pump and filter ($6k), and the landscaping water source is again operational. I tried two kinds of filters and finally chose a more expensive and reliable sand filter. As described later, we have a lawn sprinkler system and about two miles of drip hose directed to a large number of new trees and vineyard, and the filter catches dirt particles that would clog the drip system emitters.

Figure 3-4a: View of elevated building pad

Figure 3-4b: View of driveway from pad

Lessons Learned:
- Riparian rights are complicated and valuable.
- Consult a water-rights specialist.

Ground Water

Proximity to a creek may provide underground or surface water, which makes the height of the water table a concern. When we dug the surface trenches for the septic pipes and utility cables, the trenches were only about 3' deep, but quickly filled with water, indicating that the property has a high ground-water table. In summer, areas with a high water table are apparent from their lush growth of green wild grasses. This high water table causes the clay soil to expand, which makes foundation design problematic; see Chapter 4.

Lessons Learned: Identify water table levels and surface soil types.

There are also several water sources on the north side of the property, including water outlet easements from the neighboring property and runoff from the highway. This water travels to the creek on the surface or through underground culverts installed by the previous property owner. Currently a nuisance, it can be tapped for either irrigation or decorative water effects, as discussed in the Landscaping section. One initial use is for an artificial pond as shown in Figure 5-13b along with a small bridge.

Flood Plain

A creek is an asset for irrigation, but it is also a liability if the property lies mainly in the flood plain. To avoid a potential flood, the house site's building pad, shown in Figure 3-2, is situated 450 feet from Bear Creek, Figure 3-3b, on slightly higher ground (the terrain rises about 1% away from the creek), beyond the 100-year flood plain. As Chapter 4 explains further, the building pad is raised 2' using crushed shale rock, and the 36" foundation lifts the floor further. See Figure 3-4a for a view of the elevated building pad and front driveway (looking south). Nevertheless, we also have a flood insurance policy. Figure 3-4b shows the driveway and vineyard viewed from the home site, looking west.

Lessons Learned:
- Flood plain information is publicly available.
- Consult an insurance agent for flood coverage.

Power Issues

The utility company predicted my electric usage based upon the electric water-well pump's power requirement. For a fee, the utility company installed a power pole, an overhead cable, an underground cable and an aboveground transformer box; this box is just barely visible in Figure 3-4a, near the driveway in the middle of the photo. The major expense in a power installation is cable to the building site (1200' x $100/foot). See Figure 3-4b for a view of the driveway towards the power pole, and Figure 3-5b for a view of the driveway looking towards the Chateau. The utility also required an easement giving them legal access to their cables and equipment. This legally recorded document becomes a permanent requirement of successive owners, and most title reports list these easements. As described later, the placement of the electric meter posed some difficulties.

Figure 3-5a: View of septic tank near house

Figure 3-5b: View of phase 2 from tree-lined driveway

Lessons Learned:
- The power company may need an estimate of your power use.
- Consider your long-term power needs when the home is expanded.

Septic System

In a septic system, the plumbing in the house funnels wastewater to a nearby tank, shown in Figure 3-5a, from which it's distributed to the septic field. Local septic regulations require soil tests to determine the correct location for a drain field, which must have several feet of unsaturated soil beneath it. Due to the high ground-water table on my property, it was necessary to build a sand filter system. This system uses a pump to re-circulate the wastewater through a bed of sand. This type of system has no real disadvantages, other than its higher cost and its reliance on an electric pump. The septic field is 50' from the house, but the regulations require that the two underground septic tanks be close (15') to the house. Another pump gets the wastewater from this storage tank (Figure 3-5a) to the septic field. The system is sized for a six-bedroom house. Since the construction project involves an expandable building, it's practical to start with a larger septic system, which is not significantly more costly than a small system.

Lessons Learned: Size septic for the ultimate house.

Site Planning

While a city lot may not offer many options for positioning a house, a large lot allows more freedom in choosing the building's position and orientation. For my 25-acre site, I considered several factors that are particular to my project, but may be a useful point of reference to others.

Lot and Orientation

As can be seen from the site plan in Figure 3-2, the lot is a long narrow rectangle. We decided to align the rear of the house with the long direction to incorporate much of the lot in the "back yard." However, the property is so vast that it requires serious attention, and breaking the yard into zones, developed individually as if they were outside rooms. Three rows of trees were planted along the back 740' in order to screen the house property from the immediate neighbors to the south.

Privacy

Most chateaux and grand manor houses are set on large lots, isolated from other homes. In that tradition, I sought a secluded setting for Chateau Herbe. The 1,200' driveway entrance to the building provides sufficient distance from the street, and the newly planted trees that line the driveway offer screening, as shown in Figure 3-5b (looking east).

This site is isolated from most neighbors and provides mutual privacy, as can be seen in the photo in Figure 3-6a. Figure 3-6b (view from the rear of the house) shows that the phase 1 garden room protrudes to the rear (left side of photo); the phase 2 tower under construction holds the garage. The house is far from the street.

Figure 3-6a: Perspective of phase 2 garage end

Figure 3-6b: View of phase 2 site from rear lawn

Enjoying (and Improving) the View
A prominent feature in the area is Mt. Ashland, a ski resort often covered with snow. The southern exposure of the back of the house allows a fine view of the mountain from all the rear windows.

Another issue was preserving the authentic, historic character of Herbe's appearance. Built in 1630, the Norman chateau originally had no garage, although one was added to the right front of the building a few hundred years later; see Figure 1-1a. In the Herbe design, the garage is in the left tower (phase 2), close to the hillside in Figure 3-6b, with a side entrance in Figure 3-6a. The garage doors aren't visible as you approach the front of the house, eliminating a potential anachronism.

One drawback of the site is its proximity to the highway (Figure 3-6b), for reasons of noise as well as privacy. We planted about 1,000 trees and seedlings to screen neighboring properties and the highway. Water pumped from the creek irrigates the trees. We obtained permission from the Oregon Department of Transportation (ODOT) to place decorative poplar trees in a line on the strip of state land between the property and the roadway. Nearby towns have similar screenings that are quite attractive. We also planted evergreen trees to provide year-round screening. Over the years, we expect the highway to be less noticeable; meanwhile, it is somewhat noisy. An adjacent hill acts as a sound barrier, as shown in Figure 3-6b. The hill and the mass of the building itself insulate the rear of the house from the highway. Inside the house the highway can barely be heard.

If one were building a less formal style house, another site tucked into this hillside would offer more protection from the winds and from the highway. However, for the Herbe Chateau, the more isolated location was preferred.

Water-Related Issues
The Norman chateau is adjacent to a water-filled moat, as seen in Figure 1-2b. The effect is both distinctive and attractive. On the Herbe property, it would be aesthetically desirable to build the chateau next to the creek, hidden in the trees (see top of the photo in Figure 3-6a). Because of the flooding issues, however, the building site is 450' away from the creek and at a slightly higher elevation.

I also considered several ideas for a moat, but since I already have a high ground water table and am in a flood zone, it didn't seem sensible to add a body of water very close to the house. Accordingly we have a bridge in the driveway over the ponds as shown in the photo in Figure 5-13b that hint of an "ancient" moat.

Figure 3-7a: Measuring sun trajectory at site

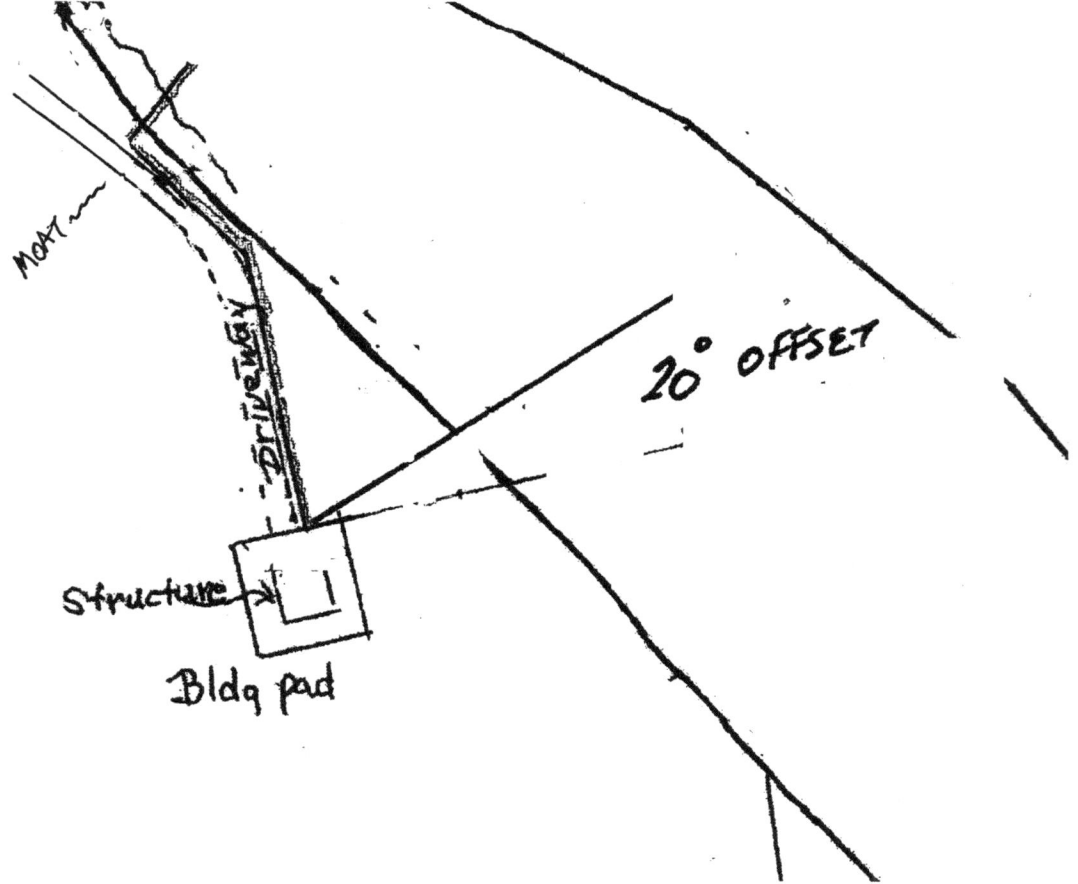

Figure 3-7b: Recording sun trajectory on site plan

Views of the Chateau
A constant view of a building while driving up to it isn't very dramatic; it's more interesting to have some change of perspective, or "apparent motion" of the object, as you approach. Many chateaux are designed with an approach that shows them to advantage; the Norman chateau takes this to the extreme, with its driveway passing left, then right, to give a view of the chateau from every perspective.

To provide a perspective of Chateau Herbe, the long 1200' driveway shown in Figure 3-4b offers a fleeting view of the house when driving from the gate to the front door. The driveway comes in at a 40-degree angle, except for the last 100' section, which approaches the building straight on, as seen in the photo of the driveway in Figure 3-4a and the site plan in Figure 3-7b.

Sunlight
In placing and orienting a house, its sun and shade exposures are an important consideration; one common arrangement has the front of the house facing north and the rear facing south to give the back of the house maximum sun. Another issue is the placement of rooms within the house plan to take advantage of sunlight. Before construction started, we took photographs, as in Figure 3-7a looking due west, to capture the sun shadows at various times of the day and year, in order to understand the sun's movement and effects on the lot.

The trajectory of the sun during the day depends upon your latitude and the date. In North America (northern latitude) the sun never quite gets directly overhead at noon, but lies to the south most of the day. By referring to some books and Internet programs, we determined the trajectory of the sun for Ashland, Oregon (latitude 42 degrees); based on that information we made some graphs and tables of the sun's behavior and recorded them on the site plan, Figure 3-7b.

Herbe's garden room is located at the back of the building to get maximum daylight, and its eight windows provide some solar heating in winter, see Figure 2-3b. To gain more "early sun" at the rear of the house, and also to protect the garden room from excessive sun on summer afternoons, the building was rotated 20 degrees counterclockwise within the building pad (from a due north/south orientation) as indicated in Figure 3-7b.

The sun's exposure was also a determining factor on the relative positions of the kitchen and dining room in the right tower (phase 3). My initial plan had the kitchen at the rear of the tower to catch the morning sun, while the dining room was in the front to catch the setting sun, as seen in the floor plan in Figure 2-1b. However, I reconsidered this during the several years of construction. When I finally specified phase 4, I swapped the kitchen and dining room, expanding the dining room to include a rear bump-out for the views to the rear of Mt. Ashland. I also added a breakfast nook at the end of the Chateau on the sunny south side; see Chapter 5 and Figure 5-13a.

Lessons Learned: Phased construction permits floor plan changes.

Figure 3-8: View of phase 2 through vineyard

Facing North

One disadvantage of the front being in the north is that it only gets the evening sun for a few months mid-summer. In classic architecture the quoins and other moldings are enhanced by the sun's shadows. Unfortunately with a north front exposure one loses this favorable shadowing effect on the trim, and consequently the front of the building isn't quite as attractive.

Lessons Learned: Rear south exposure reduces the shadows on the north elevation.

Landscaping

A prominent characteristic of most chateaux is symmetric landscaping, as shown in Figure 1-1a. Landscaping is a major expense, and I had to consider several overriding issues:

- Filtering and pumping creek water to drip and sprinkler systems
- Planting trees for privacy and to form a driveway tunnel
- Planting lawns and hedges to form geometric patterns
- Placing natural plantings at the property's periphery
- Implementing a grape vineyard

We planted a row of red oak trees along the driveway, as shown in the photo in the Figure 3-5b. A small vineyard is shown in the photo in Figure 3-8. The rear lawn and boxwood-hedge border is shown in Figure 3-6b during phase 2 construction. Each year of construction, we also improved the landscape architecture and gardens. I've gotten many ideas on formal French gardens from books and landscape professionals. See also vendors' comments in Chapter 6.

Lessons Learned:
- Landscaping is a major expense, but adds charm to the site.
- Strategic plantings are rewarding in the long term.
- A reliable irrigation system requires professional help.

Figure 4-1a: View of foundation piers

Figure 4-1b: View of grade beam rebar connections

Chapter 4
Foundation and Building Materials

ne advantage of a multi-stage construction project is learning from mistakes made in early phases. The quirks of novel building materials and problems with a site are discussed in this chapter as examples of lessons learned.

Engineered Foundation
The high percentage of clay on Herbe's building site makes the soil expand and contract, so a foundation or a footing would buckle as the soil underneath moved up and down, which was not acceptable. We considered several types of engineered foundations to overcome the soil weakness: augers, piles and piers. While the self-tapping auger is often an excellent approach, it requires solid soil to "bite" into, and hence is not suited for a site with a high water table. Driving posts into bedrock is a better solution; we considered the options of driving steel piles or drilling and placing concrete piers. Here the issue of multi-phase construction was the deciding factor; the cost of moving a large pile-driver rig to the site is approximately $5,000, which would be acceptable as a one-time cost, i.e., if the house, with its 100 piles, was being built all at once, and the cost could be averaged to about $50 per pile. However, since the house was being built in several stages, a more scalable solution, with lower fixed costs, was needed, even if the total cost for the entire project were ultimately higher. Hence, I opted for concrete piers, which could be installed in phases.

Lessons Learned:
- Evaluate soils to judge foundation costs.
- Some phased solutions aren't economical.

Piers
A well driller installed 20' steel pipes 3' into bedrock; they protrude about 1' above ground, as shown in Figure 4-1a. The pipes, 10.75" in diameter, were placed using a conventional drilling rig; also see Chapter 6. Each building phase requires about 25 of these $700 piers, at 5' intervals along the base of the block walls.

The pipes are fitted with steel rebar (reinforcing bar) cages, then filled with concrete. Pouring wet concrete down a 20' pipe is problematic, as the rock tends to separate out of the concrete mixture as it falls, which weakens the structure; adding to the problem, the cages had horizontal crosspieces, which prohibited running the line pump's nozzle through the pipe. A consultant addressed this problem with a cumbersome ball flow valve, and as a result the pour took six hours to complete. In phase 2 we redesigned the cages to simplify the pour.

Lessons Learned: Build steel cages to accommodate a pump's nozzle.

Figure 4-2a: View of poured grade beam in forms

Figure 4-2b: View of first course blocks

Grade Beam Foundation

The foundation that sits on top of the piers is called a grade beam; the ground does not support it. The concrete and steel beam supporting Herbe is about 16" thick and 36" tall. Figure 4-1b shows the steel rebar to be embedded in the grade beam, tied to the pier's steel cage before the grade beam is framed. Note that the vertical steel coming out of the pier is bent 90 degrees and tied parallel to the grade beam steel.

As an extra precaution, the foundation's designer specified that the bottom of the grade beam should be V-shaped to guide any moving soil around the beam rather than having it push up. Figure 4-1b shows a Styrofoam form proposed in phase 1 to create this V shape; an inspector rejected this idea. In phase 2, compacted sand formed the groove into which the concrete was poured — a lesson learned.

Lessons Learned: Local inspectors might not accept novel ideas.

The photo in Figure 4-2a shows the poured grade beam still in the plywood framing, as in conventional foundations. The protruding vertical rebar's in the grade beam are spaced 15" apart to match the pitch of the cavity cells in the wall's blocks; wood guides keep the beam's rebar in line and vertical in the wet concrete. Of course, the beam's top surface needs to be level so that the building is straight, and modern laser leveling tools and nailed markers help with this task.

Blocked in the exterior of the grade beam is a 12" frame for a granite nameplate. It was easy to get a custom nameplate engraved with "Herbe II" (See Figure 6-1a) from a company that makes gravestones. For decoration, and to simulate large stone blocks used in ancient chateaux, the face of the grade beam has a beveled top edge. To further the stone block illusion, vertical beveled cuts are made in the grade beam at 24" intervals. These cuts are visible in Figure 1-8a. It's easy to achieve such effects by adding molding on the inside of the forms from the beginning.

Lessons Learned: Plan for foundation decoration prior to setting the forms.

Insulated Concrete Forms

Available from a number of vendors, and used most often for foundation framing, Insulated Concrete Forms (ICFs) made of polystyrene are discarded once the poured concrete has set. Our foundation subcontractor preferred conventional plywood framing as shown in the photos for the grade beam, but all the outer walls are made from ICFs. The photo in Figure 4-2b shows the first course of 15" blocks, with rebar protruding up through their empty cells, sitting directly upon the grade beam after the wood forms have been removed. Note that on the lower left a wood shim is being used to level a block on the grade beam (later concrete filled this space).

The floor joists attach to a plate on the grade beam, providing a 36" crawl space under the first floor. The grade beam's 16" thickness accommodates: 10" for the block thickness, 4" for the joist's foundation plate, and an extra 2" outside of the block. The crawl space is accessible through a trap door-- typically in a first floor closet.

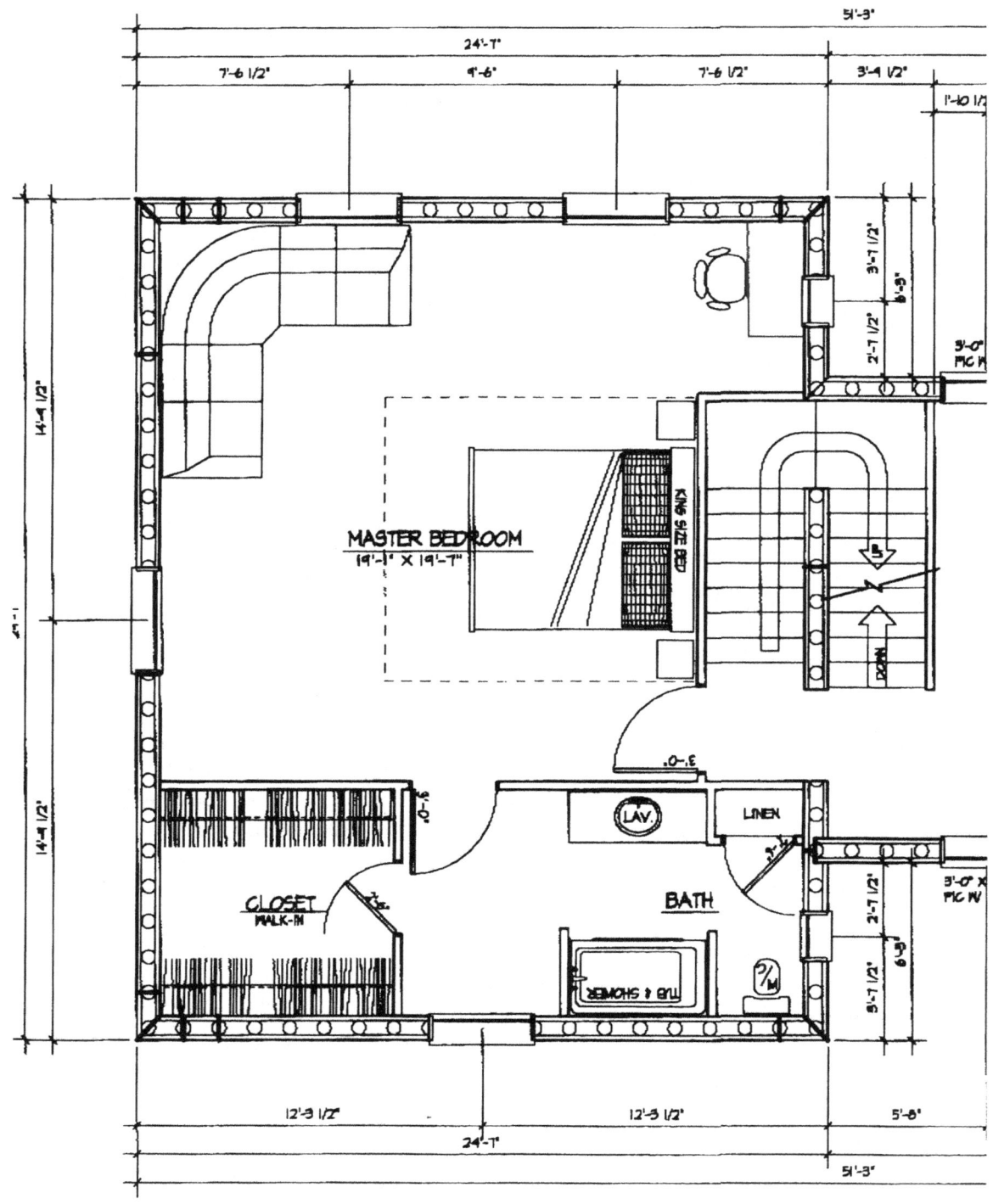

Figure 4-3: Designer's sample floor plan

Designing With Blocks
All of Herbe's outer walls and interior load-bearing walls are made of RASTRA® ("Rastra") cavity ICF blocks that consist of 85% recycled Styrofoam and 15% concrete. The block manufacturer provided me with a list of designers familiar with its products. Relying on the designer's expertise in using ICF blocks should put you further along the learning curve, and consequently reduce your risk. See Chapter 6 for vendor's comments.

The nearest design firm was a few hundred miles from my building site, but as most of the communication would be done by fax and email, this wasn't a problem. As shown in Figure 4-3, the designer's floor plan of a Herbe tower bedroom, the 10"-thick ICF walls are drawn to scale and show the position of the 6" circular concrete cavity cells on 15" spacing, and suggested miter cuts. Walls should end with a concrete cell, so the best length is a multiple of 15" if the corners are to be mitered or an additional 10" if not; it's best to find a designer familiar with these details. The (non-load-bearing) interior walls are conventional 4" stick framing and drawn accordingly.

Lessons Learned: Choose a designer familiar with the building materials.

To develop my plan, the designer converted my (faxed) floor plans into the detailed design drawings, as shown in the tower bedroom in Figure 4-3. The designer made preliminary decisions on types and sizes of materials, beams and joists; the ICF block vendor's design guide suggested the techniques for connecting the blocks to other fixtures. Planning departments require plans to have the official stamp of a registered architect or an engineer A structural engineer reviewed the construction plans and then made the final choices that were incorporated into the finished plan. This extra communication took some time.

Lessons Learned: Coordinate among various subcontractors.

While we did not have problems with the local building authorities because of our choice of building materials, such issues can arise. The building associations have standard approval codes. Ultimately, if the manufacturer has secured these approvals, local building departments will accept their products. However, planners may raise questions that might not occur with conventional materials. See Chapter 6 on ICBO approvals.

Building With Blocks
Finding a contract framer experienced with the ICF blocks was more difficult than finding a designer; there were a few in Oregon, but none in the town of Ashland. Builders recommended by the block manufacturer gave me some brief advice by telephone. An Arizona builder close to the "pour" stage of his project invited me to visit his site. So in 1997 my wife, Maurine, and I spent a weekend in Phoenix AZ., took a quick tour of the house under construction, and took some photographs to document some of the ICF building techniques (Figure 1-7). Finally, I found a contractor in Ashland willing to learn about the blocks. An experienced builder in Eugene (100 miles away) who had a few extra blocks to sell agreed to come down to my site, set the first course of blocks (Figure 4-2b), and provide a short tutorial to my contractor. The Rastra customer support group provided a guidebook to get my builder up to speed. See Chapter 6 for my contractor's comments.

Figure 4-4a: View of foam block delivery

Figure 4-4b: View of phase 2 block framing

Building Materials - Insulated Concrete Forms

The blocks provide insulation as well as the interior and exterior wall surface; they are similar to conventional concrete cinder blocks, except that they are glued together rather than set with mortar. The blocks have 6" holes that are filled with liquid concrete. This block is 10" thick; it's available in 9' and 10' lengths, and 15" (single) and 30" (double) height. ICF blocks cost about $50 each. An advantage of the smaller block is that two people can manipulate its 150 pounds; however, using a crane on larger blocks reduces the number of blocks to be placed. My crane rental costs were up to $2,000 per month, an added expense of multi-story building.

Lessons Learned: Locate an inexpensive crane with a certified operator.

The blocks' 6"-diameter holes are spaced every 15", running both vertically and horizontally, so the poured concrete creates a 2-dimensional web, providing structural integrity. These holes are visible in Figure 4-4a, showing a flatbed truck arriving at the job site. A forklift, fitted with an adapter for the block holes, unloaded the truck.

The photo in Figure 4-4b shows the phase 2 first floor framed with glued blocks. Blocks can be turned 90 degrees and placed either horizontally or vertically, as shown near the right side of the photo. Each block ends with a 3" half-cell, completed with the half-cell of the mating block (or cemented to the foundation). Blocks can be miter cut to mate with another block, or two blocks can merge at right angles. Figure 4-3, lower right corner, illustrates a mitered connection, whereas just above it is a right angle merge of blocks.

Blocks can be easily cut with a hand saw (Figure 6-4a) or with a chain saw. It's important to maintain the integrity of the alignment of the cavity cells so that the formed concrete columns are continuous. Window holds can either be cut out or framed with block from the start, as in Figure 4-4b. Although I had planned on a window in the garage tower, and you can see what looks like a partial doorway in Figure 4-4b, I changed my mind during the framing, and decided to eliminate this window. It was a simple matter for the construction workers to re-fill the opening with block pieces glued in as a patch.

Reinforcing steel (rebar) is set both horizontally and vertically within the cell cavities prior to the concrete pouring. Because Herbe was built in multiple phases it was necessary to add exterior blocks connected to an already built (and poured) structure. To accommodate this my contractors drilled holes into the already set block, and epoxy-glued rebar connectors to join into the newly set (un-poured) ICF blocks. Figure 1-8a illustrates an addition during the phase 2 construction.

Novel Product Problems

Near the end of our framing we ran out of blocks, and were, of course, unable to run down to the local building-supply store and pick up a few extra. As a result we had to scrounge to find some extra blocks and pay a freight bill to get them.

Lessons Learned: Novel products may not be available locally; order extra.

Figure 4-5a: View of interior block wall

Figure 4-5b: View of joists at ledger beam

ICF Wall Section

A partially completed interior ICF wall section is shown in Figure 4-5a, in which the horizontal 6" cells filled with concrete are plainly visible; the vertical cells are also filled, and the vertical rebar indicates these concrete cell locations. The U-shaped stairwell, built of wood, is bolted to the block's concrete cells. To save stairwell space, an extra step was squeezed between the two landings, and this 11" tread fairly matches to the 10" thick ICF block as shown in the photo, as per the floor plan in Figure 5-5. The adjacent second-floor joists and sheeting are also visible in this photo.

The interfacing of second-floor BCI Joists® to the ICF blocks is shown in Figure 4-5b. Heavy 4"x12" ledger boards are placed around the interior sides of the walls and are bolted into the empty cells before the concrete is poured. The joists are nailed to this ledger board with conventional metal joist hangers. With joists installed and some sheeting plywood laid, the pump operator can walk above the braced wall tops to fill the block cells with concrete. Also note the leveling shims protruding from the wall in Figure 4-5b.

A building inspector is experienced in checking for compliance with local building codes, but may raise new issues when presented with novel materials. As an example, many building codes require that that the ledger beam that supports the floor joists must be at least 4" thick. Steel bolts connect the ledger beam to the ICF wall; their spacing and configuration need to be approved. An engineering drawing provides the details for the builder and the inspector.

Temporary Wall Support

The Styrofoam blocks provide little structural support until concrete is placed and set within the wall cavities. While a glued ICF block wall might look strong, bracing is required until the concrete is placed. A glued wall fell down in heavy winds due to inadequate bracing. Sturdy wooden vertical support posts and diagonal braces are needed as temporary support for the ledgers, as shown in Figure 4-5b, prior to pouring the concrete into the blocks. Extra bracing to hold the corners together and support the ledger beams adds to the labor and material costs of using ICF blocks. (This is not obvious when looking at a completed ICF wall after the bracing is removed.)

Window Bucks

Other block shapes are available, such as 2" flat stock. These were used for trim and some window frames, as in Figure 4-5b. This window frame prevents liquid concrete from escaping the block during the concrete pour. However, in seating a window it's better to create some extra space for a concrete frame rather than using pieces of foam block as if it were made of wood, see Figure 4-9a. Figure 4-6b shows the bucks for the garage doors. Figure 4-10c shows a finished window framed with block.

Figure 4-6a: View of line pump for blocks

Figure 4-6b: View of overhead pump

Concrete Pour - An Exciting Event

After the blocks are glued together, and with exterior braces holding the walls in place, steel rebar is threaded through the empty cells horizontally and vertically, visible in Figure 4-6a. Building corners get L-shaped horizontal rebar — this is somewhat tricky to place after the blocks are all glued together; we laid them in with each block course.

After the first floor was framed to a height of 11', concrete was poured down each of the wall's cells. We used a conventional line pump, as in Figure 4-6a; it is noteworthy to compare the size of the man's elbow with the size of the block and its cavity. (See also Figure 6-5.) We also tried an overhead pump. Although more expensive, the overhead pump is more convenient in getting the hose routed to the proper position, as shown in Figure 4-6b, but the extra pressure may increase the likelihood of a blowout (see below). Every couple of minutes the operator re-positions to the next column of block cavities to place the liquid concrete. Since it's fairly wet, the concrete flows slightly to the adjacent cell on each side. We made several trips around the perimeter filling the cells with concrete in stages. Rebar was used as a stirring rod at the top to eliminate air bubbles. It's important to check that the concrete is filling the blocks, and I watched an expert puncture the blocks to make spot checks.

Windows and doors need wood frames to hold back the wet concrete. These may be temporary bucks, as shown for the garage doors in Figure 4-6b, or a permanent frame for an exterior pre-hung door. To ensure that the concrete flows across a windowsill, small holes are made in the block under the sill; or, the top wood sill is placed after the concrete is poured beneath it. A few days after the first floor was poured, the second floor blocks were framed above the first floor; the second-floor concrete was poured a few weeks later. Note the vertical rebar projecting out the top of the first floor blocks to mate to the next course of blocks in the phase 2 photo in Figure 4-6b.

One hazard while pouring concrete is a blowout — i.e., something "gives," allowing wet concrete to leak out. This happened during the second floor pour; the problem was quickly remedied by applying a piece of plywood to hold back the concrete. As a precaution on the upper floor, small plywood panels were clamped using all-thread rods to hold the blocks together, as shown in the photo. This advance effort averts problems in precarious spots.

Lessons Learned: Be prepared during a concrete pour to patch a blowout.

Most chateaux have a mansard roof — i.e. a tilted wall (steep roof pitch) that provides the top floor of living space or "super attic." In the Herbe design the first two floors are framed using ICF blocks, and the third floor is built of wood using two parallel beams and scissor rafters to form a gambrel style roof that looks like a barn. This roofline end isn't chateau-like, but was very easy to extend and was hidden when the towers were added; see the photo of the roof end in Figure 4-6b.

Figure 4-7a: View of electric wiring within block wall

Figure 4-7b: View of cabinet supports within block wall

Electrical and Fixture Attachment

Figure 4-7a shows the installation of a wall switch and an outlet in a block wall. The fixture boxes are glued into cavities dug out of the 9"-wide block cavities. The ROMEX® wiring can go anywhere, since it's placed within the 2" outer surface of the 10"-thick block. The electrician used a chain saw to create these wiring channels, visible in the photo as white lines. In most cases sheetrock covered over the block cavities.

To hang cabinets and other heavy objects, we glued 2"x4"s into wall cavities and used bolts set into the concrete cavity cells. These boards are set flush with the wall surface to provide a convenient nailing interface. Figure 4-7b shows the end of the foyer in which the wet bar (phase 1 kitchen) wall cabinets will be mounted. It's helps to place these boards during the early stages of framing, so it helps to have the cabinet plans finished early.

Lessons Learned: Place integrated wooden supports prior to concrete pour.

Interior Finishes

The interior side of the ICF blocks can be painted, covered with conventional sheet rock or paneling, or plastered. Hand-applied plaster is labor intensive and expensive, but provides a finished surface reminiscent of authentic finishes in chateaux. We found glued sheet rock the most cost-effective treatment.

The living room and dining room had fancier paneling, but to simplify the attachment we generally first used sheetrock and then applied MDF wooden panels or fine grade plywood. See Chapter 5 for more interior finishing information.

Styrofoam Arches

Prefabricated foam arches, another useful product, were used inside of all the arched windows. These foam trim pieces come in various sizes and are covered with sheet-rock paper covering. Foam arches are also useful in fabricating doorway entries. There is a trimmed arch top over the 60"-wide doorway between the foyer and the garden room. See the photo in Figure 4-7b, and Figure 4-8a looking towards the front doorway from inside the garden room.

Although many of the interior walls are done with stick construction, this first floor interior wall is an exterior wall to the salon above, and was therefore built of ICF blocks. The foam arches can be used with both ICF and conventional wood walls, and can be purchased in semicircular or elliptical patterns. An alternative to using these prefabricated arches is to build an arch out of plywood and then to apply wet, grooved sheetrock. These traditional methods are more labor-intensive than using the prefabricated pieces.

Figure 4-8a: View of prefab arch in doorway

Figure 4-8b: View of front stucco application

Exterior Stucco

Many types of exterior finish can be applied to the exterior of the ICF blocks. We chose stucco, which normally would be painted, but the rougher look of the raw stucco is more authentic for Herbe's first phase. Since Rastra block contains 15% concrete, its rough surface accepts stucco directly, eliminating the tarpaper or wonder board necessary in conventional wood-framed construction.

Our finishing contractor recommended artificial stucco, which was applied by hand, in two coats — a scratch coat followed by a thicker finishing coat — as shown in Figure 4-8b. The synthetic stucco isn't completely waterproof, but provides a hard surface. Hand-applied stucco is expensive; a cheaper alternative is to spray the stucco using a pump system similar to swimming pool construction. Our vendor also pushed a plastic mesh into the wet stucco surface for added dimensional stability. We applied latex paint after phase 4 was done.

Trim

The Norman chateau has considerable exterior trim. In Herbe, we used ICF flat-stock material to fabricate most of the exterior trim, quoins, window surrounds and windowsills shown in Figure 4-8b. The flat stock is easy to cut with a handsaw or shape with a rasp. Custom-making these parts was cheaper than buying pre-cast stone trim. On the other hand, the interior window surround trim uses pre-made fluted 3½" molding pieces that are convenient but expensive.

Doors and Windows

Many chateaux have glass-paned French doors. A typical pair of doors is 60" wide and 80" high, and may have a transom window above. The Norman chateau (Figure 1-1b) uses similar doors, with safety railings, as windows on each side of the center door. Rather than this, Herbe's 42" wide front door is wood/glass, with exterior grids and arched transom shown in Figure 4-8. On both sides of Herbe's front, there are arched picture windows, rather than doors. These windows are less expensive ($500) than doors ($900). Doors require more expensive tempered glass, and because of their size require more framing material around them, which reduces the amount of visible window area. Since doors need to open, their seal is not perfect, and they sometimes warp.

These two picture windows are 42" wide, 72" tall with a 21" arch, giving a total height of 93" — a little smaller than in Normandy. Windows with interior grids are easier to clean than partitioned windows, and vinyl window frames are less expensive than wood. Picture windows are also less expensive than operating windows, and have a better seal. I opted for thicker glass for better insulation.

A window can look similar to a pair of French doors, but is less expensive; however, its grid pattern may differ from that of a door, as can be seen in Figure 4-8b. Low windows present problems. Some building codes require that windows located within 18" of the floor use safer and more expensive tempered glass. However, if a window's pane area is less than nine square feet, tempered glass may not be required. My picture window has two rectangular halves separated by a "T" bar that reduces the glass area of each panel and eliminates the requirement for tempered glass.

Figure 4-9a: View of arched window installation

Figure 4-9b: View of rear deck balustrade

Lessons Learned: Check building codes for window requirements.

Arched Window Framing

Arched windows are available with a variety of sunburst sectional schemes, but none that matched the Normandy pattern. Our window vendor customized the grid pattern to match those in the original chateau, and provided much of the expertise in selecting the style and type of windows (Figure 4-9a).

Framing arched windows in the block was a problem! Most vinyl windows have a 1" installation fin on the sides for nailing to a frame; this is not very useful with the blocks, as nails won't hold in Styrofoam, unless wooden buck surrounds are embedded in the window cutouts. Instead, our carpenters made oversized rectangular cutouts in the block for the 36"-wide picture windows in the garden room. They then glued in pieces of the ICF flat stock as window stops, as shown in Figure 4-9a. They also cut and glued small block pieces to hold the arched window tops in place. Cutting and gluing ICF is labor-intensive, similar to the way windows would have been "bricked" in antiquity. As mentioned earlier the exterior decorative window surrounds were custom made of ICF flat stock.

The third-floor dormer windows shown in Figure 4-9b have hand-carved wooden exterior surrounds. The elk horn motif matches the original chateau. In phase 2 we made a rubber mold and cast all six surrounds using a polymer material.

Balustrade

The center section of Herbe's rear balcony, shown in Figure 4-9b, contains pre-cast concrete balusters that weigh about 60 pounds each. These are commercially available at about $40 apiece. When I picked up the 24 balusters at the manufacturer in San Jose, California, in a half-ton pickup truck, I didn't realize that the load of balusters actually weighed just slightly less than a ton. The drive to Oregon was slow and perilous.

Building codes specify the wall height as 36" or 42" and impose a difficult requirement — that there cannot be an opening larger than 4", to prevent babies and children from getting their heads stuck between the balusters. As a result, the balusters had to be set very close together. Most of the old estates have their balusters set much further apart; unfortunately, modern codes don't allow this.

Each baluster has rebar running through it top to bottom; the rebar protrudes a couple of inches on each end for mounting. Base and wall cap tops, made of either concrete or synthetic, are available for mounting the balusters. We used the vendor's standard balustrade base. The rear balcony (two 15" tall ICF blocks) is shown in Figure 4-10a prior to installing the balusters. There is a small concrete formed base to hold the base cap for the balusters. Perhaps we could have simply drilled and set the balusters on this base.

Figure 4-10a: View of rear second floor deck

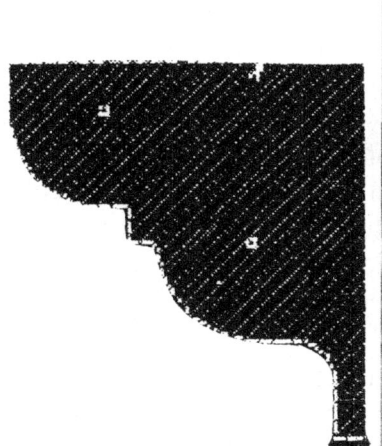

Figure 4-10b:
Corbel profile pattern

Figure 4-10c: View of tower fascia box and corbels

Extruded Styrofoam
To get a more comfortable rounded top on the deck railing and above the balustrade, rather than buying a pre-cast concrete cap, I designed a custom, inexpensive extruded Styrofoam wall cap. The Figure 4-9b photo shows this wall cap glued on top of the ICF balcony wall and balustrade. The underside of this cap holds a piece of pressure-treated wood, drilled to accept the baluster rod. Later this foam cap was covered with fiberglass and stucco.

Custom extruded Styrofoam moldings are available from a number of vendors. Using your custom, constant cross-sectional pattern, an 8'-long piece of Styrofoam is pushed through a hot-wire former. In Herbe's construction there were many uses for these inexpensive ($4/foot) custom moldings. Custom extruded Styrofoam molding was used for the trim between the top of the rear wall and the roof. The phase 2 roof corbels are also made of extruded Styrofoam; when covered with fiberglass and stucco, this soft Styrofoam should be able to survive the rigors of the outdoors. Figure 4-10b shows a corbel profile used as the vendor's pattern. These custom made corbels, 22" x 24" x 10" thick ($20/each), are purely decorative in our designs (Figure 4-10c). In antiquity they were structural supports.

Deck Surface
Above the garden room is a 30' x 13' deck accessible from the den through French doors. The deck surface shown in Figure 4-10a is a novel rubber material. It's rolled on as a liquid in successive layers and sand is sprinkled over it, producing a surface that's waterproof and quite durable. Deck flashing is necessary but problematic. Experts suggested a combination of flashing forming an overlap at the wall/deck interface.

Roof
Most chateaux have tile, slate, or copper roofs. For economy, we used conventional asphalt shingles with a 40-year warranty and with a high definition pattern, as seen in Figure 4-10c. The black color is suitable for my application. The "stealth" vent is barely visible near the top, and all plumbing vents are concealed on the rear roof. Unlike classic chateaux, I have no chimneys protruding through the roof as all of my fireplaces are electric.

Heating and Air Conditioning
I chose a less commonly used, in-ground heat pump; there's a vinyl-tubing coil buried 5' underground where the temperature is a constant 55 degrees. Cooling is more efficient because of the wider thermal differential: the temperature difference between 80 degrees in the house and 55 degrees underground is large (25 degrees). By contrast, on a hot day an aboveground heat pump has a negative 15-degree differential (80-95 degrees). Although an in-ground system costs more to install (e.g. $18k vs. $10k), it should save money and energy in the long run. The high ground-water table that hurts foundation design and landscaping activities provides good heat conduction and is an excellent "heat sink" for the HVAC system — finally, the high water table is an advantage.

Figure 5-1a: Front view during phase 2

Figure 5-1b: View of phase 1 blocks

Chapter 5
Construction Phases

As noted in Chapter 1, it was a primary goal of this project to "grow a chateau" in stages. Chateau Herbe was constructed in four phases over 6+ years, and the details of each of these construction phases are described chronologically in this chapter. There are a number of options for the scope and sequence of those stages, and an architectural design must consider the building materials to be used in making those choices. In the case of Herbe, the decision to use concrete required that the house be built in adjacent left/right sections rather than vertical sections. Another benefit of staged construction was learning some lessons in the first phase that would help in the later phases.

In late 1999, we started the chateau's center, an 1,800-square-foot, three-story, 2-bedroom, 2½-bath home, as shown on the right side of Figure 5-1a. The second phase, construction of the 3,000-square-foot left wing and tower, got underway one year after the center section had been finished and occupied. The left side of the photo in Figure 5-1a shows phase 2 before the stucco was applied. The third phase, the symmetric right wing and tower, was designed in 2004 and built in 2005, as described at the end of this chapter.

False Start
In 1996 I completed plans for a building similar to that shown in Figure 5-1a. The structural engineer designed the foundation using steel piles. After receiving price quotations for various aspects of the construction I concluded that building a 4,500-square-foot, three-story house, with a garage and study, all at once, exceeded both my budget and my needs for a summer home. I needed to find a less expensive starting point for my expandable home. Thereafter, I developed plans for a downsized phase 1, comprising only the center section, eliminating the left wing and tower. The redesign process added to the cost of the project.

Lessons Learned: Partitioning a design and establishing the construction sequence is costly; having to repeat the process is even more costly.

Getting Started
In mid-1998 we made major improvements to the site infrastructure and contracted with a designer to develop a new set of plans for the downsized first-phase design. The major changes were the use of concrete piers instead of steel piles, and the use of ICF blocks. While waiting for the structural engineering and permit approval, we completed the water well and power installation that were convenient to have available to the construction crew. We obtained permits for construction, and began in earnest in October 1999.

Figure 5-1b shows the first floor front as of December 1999 using the Rastra blocks. The front porch steps are not yet built, the interfacing rebar is facing the front, and an empty plywood form is lying on the ground as a safety standoff. Bracing of the ICF is evident.

Figure 5-2: View of third floor framing

Table 2:
Phase 1 History

06/99	Site prep, driveway, water well
07/99	Power installed
08/99	Plans completed
09/99	Building permit issued
10/99	Drill and set piers and cages; place pier cement
11/99	Grade beam and first course blocks set; floor joists set
12/99	First floor blocks; first floor concrete pour; second floor joists
01/00	Second floor blocks; second concrete pour; third floor joists/frame
02/00	Frame/sheet roof; back porch; windows/doors; plumbing
03/00	Exterior trim; electrical wiring; HVAC
04/00	Exterior stucco; interior sheetrock
05/00	Plaster; cabinets; paint; finish plumbing
06/00	Paint; foyer tile; interior trim; moldings; appliances
07/00	Paint; kitchen tile; carpet; landscaping; stucco rear porch
08/00	Front and rear railings; interior stairwell railing

Documenting the Process

Herbe phase 1 was completed in about one year; Table 2 shows the major steps.

To the casual observer of a construction site, progress appears to be very slow and uneven. Fortunately I got a time-lapse photographer's view! Since I live 500 miles from the construction site, an associate took semi-monthly videos and photos to keep me informed. These videotapes, archived from important phase 1 construction sequences, allowed us to make the same steps more efficient in phase 2 in many cases.

We also took hundreds of photographs to record the locations of plumbing pipes and electrical wires, and of the extra framing for future doors or additions. The photos, as in Figure 5-2, are valuable in subsequent construction phases, when it's important to know these details to avoid costly mistakes. This phase 1 view of the third floor shows the scissor rafters, the side gambrel beam, and the mansard roof rafters. At the right end you will find a pre-framed doorway and header for future phase 3 connection; the temporary vertical center stud would be cut out if a doorway were needed.

Lessons Learned: Document structural elements to simplify later additions.

My contractor and I communicated mainly by phone, but we also met face-to-face about once a month. Generally we were able to correct "mistakes" or make changes, but in a couple of cases I was resigned to accepting what had already been done. With mobile videophones, I'd expect more success in building remotely.

Foundation Piers

Since poor soil conditions required an engineered foundation, we opted for a pier system, using steel pipes installed by a conventional well-drilling rig. In placing the 22 pipes for phase 1, the driller tried several different techniques that were videotaped for the benefit of the phase 2 driller. While these tapes might be of little value to a layperson, an experienced drilling professional understands what's being documented, and can probably suggest improvements.

Similarly, the trial-and-error process of filling these pipes with concrete, as described earlier, pointed to a need for improvement in phase 2. We learned from our phase 1 mistakes, in both drilling the piers and in the design of their rebar cages, and as a result, considerable pain and labor were saved in phase 2.

Lessons Learned: In rebar cage design, consider the size of the concrete pump hose.

Another type of foundation sometimes used is a rubble trench — dig a large trench, fill it with compacted rock, and rest a concrete footing on top. This approach is suited to single-story houses, where the vertical load is relatively small. However, a three-story building needs something stronger, and so we didn't try a trench.

Lessons Learned: Consult experts in designing foundations.

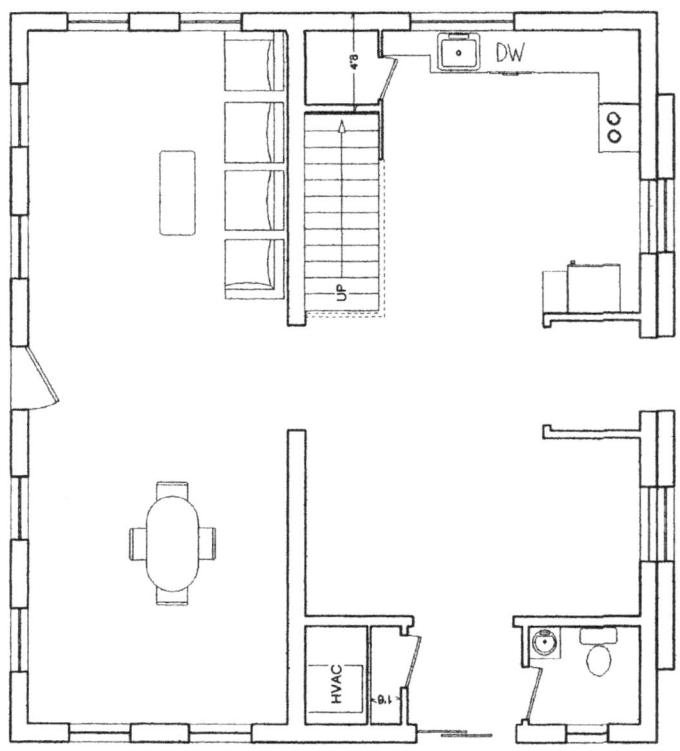

Figure 5-3a: First floor plan for phase 1

Figure 5-3b: View of phase 1 foyer/kitchen

Phase 1 Construction

Floor plan

After visiting Normandy in 1997, I revised Herbe's footprint to better reflect the proportions of the tower and wing of the original chateau. New plans were drawn for the first construction phase, giving more interim space while providing for later upgrades. Figure 5-3a shows this simplified floor plan. Figure 5-3b is a late construction photo showing the partially completed stairway and kitchen. The key differences between the subset phase 1 floor plan and the full plan for Chateau Herbe (Figure 2-2a) are:

- A stove is added in the interim kitchen in the foyer's wet bar area
- The sink is placed in the future doorway to the phase 3 living room
- The foyer's closet partitions are not installed
- The second powder room off the foyer isn't implemented
- The foyer left side door in phase 1 is an exterior door
- The second-floor salon is an interim master bedroom
- The second-floor powder room must have a shower in phase 1

Interim Kitchen

One major decision was whether to exactly maintain the eventual chateau's wet-bar footprint for the interim mini-kitchen (to minimize plumbing changes in later phases), or to build a better kitchen from the beginning. We chose the latter, as my wife favored the bigger kitchen shown in the photos in Figures 5-3b and in Figure 6-3a, showing the final interim kitchen with the decorative tile backsplash installed.

This involved a tradeoff: the sink was placed in the future doorway to the living room, which absolutely required moving the plumbing when the right wing was added. But, since plumbing is accessible from the crawl space below the kitchen and foyer, the changes were expected to be relatively easy. See Figures 2-5a and 4-7b for earlier photos of the kitchen.

No Foyer Closets

Two closets are included in plans for Chateau Herbe's foyer. We postponed installing these closets in phase 1 to leave space for an office in the front left window. Instead, a temporary closet was made in the HVAC room with a removable plywood partition, shown in the floor plan in Figure 5-3a. The electric water heater and well water pressure tank are under the stairwell and accessed via custom door panels, and the pantry is to the left of the sink.

Salon

The second-floor salon of phase 2 is used as the master bedroom in phase 1. The main difference is the addition of three large closets, which in subsequent phases could be removed or converted into a combination bar and entertainment center (Figure 5-5b). Since this is the interim master bedroom, the bathroom is equipped with a shower that otherwise wouldn't be needed. A small laundry (W/D) is adjacent to the bathroom, and the future doorway (to phase 2) is used for a clothes hamper (Figure 5-5b floor plan).

Figure 5-4a: View of rear porch

Figure 5-4b: View of phase 2 garage

Garden Room

In phase 1 the 33'-long garden room accommodates the dining and living rooms, with only the furnishings defining those functions, as shown in Figure 5-3a. Later, the garden room could be redecorated or painted with a garden motif. See Figures 2-3b and 6-6a for photos of the garden room, and Figure 5-4a for a close-up of the rear porch and garden room.

Lessons Learned: Furniture can define room function.

Powder Room Window

The ground-floor powder room at the end of the phase 1 building (Figure 5-3a) has a small window at the side of the building for ventilation and light. (Placing the window at the front of the building would have been more functional, but would have marred the building front's appearance.) In phase 2, the wall containing this window became an interior wall. (See Figure 1-8a, in which this small powder room window is visible, and the new addition in progress.) Since building codes require that bathrooms have either an opening window or a fan for ventilation, the phase 1 bathroom construction included a fan in anticipation of the removal of that window. Also, to increase living space in phase 1, the second powder room at the rear of the foyer was also deferred.

Lessons Learned:
- Consider window and door locations in expansion plans.
- Bathrooms require fans if windows are eliminated.

Usability of Phase 1

The 1,800-square-foot house was quite adequate. Seeing the kitchen from the foyer was informal and a surprise to guests, given the neoclassic front. We took most of our meals in the garden room because of the wonderful views. A small office desk and computer were placed in the front foyer window, and the light and view out the front were pleasant while working there. The barbecue and chairs on the rear porch behind the garden room were a great advantage, even in winter (Figure 5-4a). The bedrooms on the second and third floor are very fine. The second floor deck was pleasant and we often kept its rear door open.

The biggest deficiency of this phase was the lack of a garage, and the inconvenience of having to climb 18 steps after leaving your reading glasses in the bedroom. The heating and air conditioning were excellent and the sound insulation was good. We had a leak to the attic that allowed bees to enter the third-floor bathroom.

ICF Block quality varied slightly depending upon the vendor. We've had no problems with the blocks, but have noticed some spider cracking in the stucco surface. The seals on two windows broke, and the manufacturer replaced the glazing under warranty.

One year's experience with the site, foundation, construction techniques, and lessons learned gave me confidence to proceed with the second phase improvements, including a two-car garage (Figure 5-4b). I had also gained experience with a group of subcontractors, and they in turn were familiar with my site and my construction materials. This added to my confidence and reduced my risk in building the next phase.

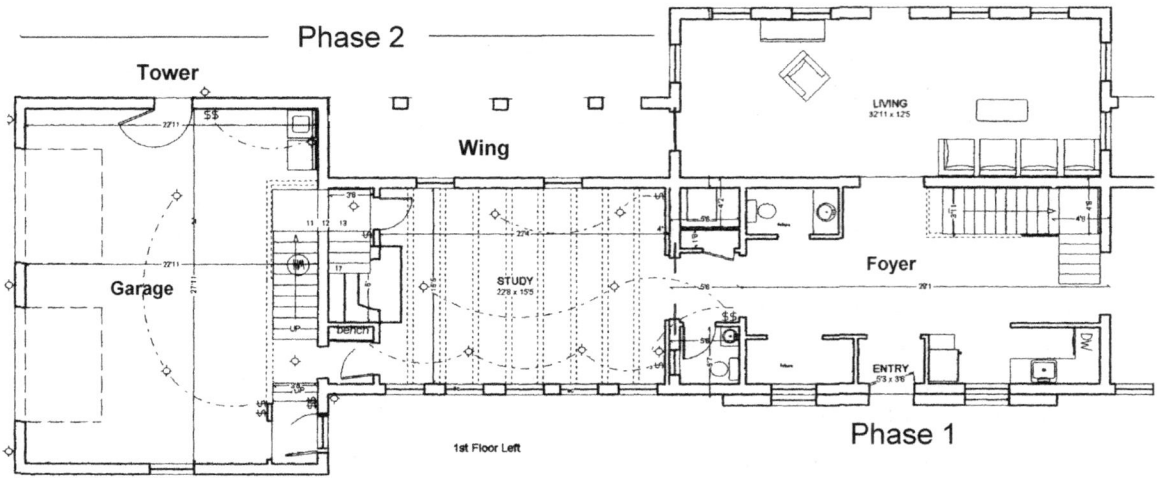

Figure 5-5a: First floor plan

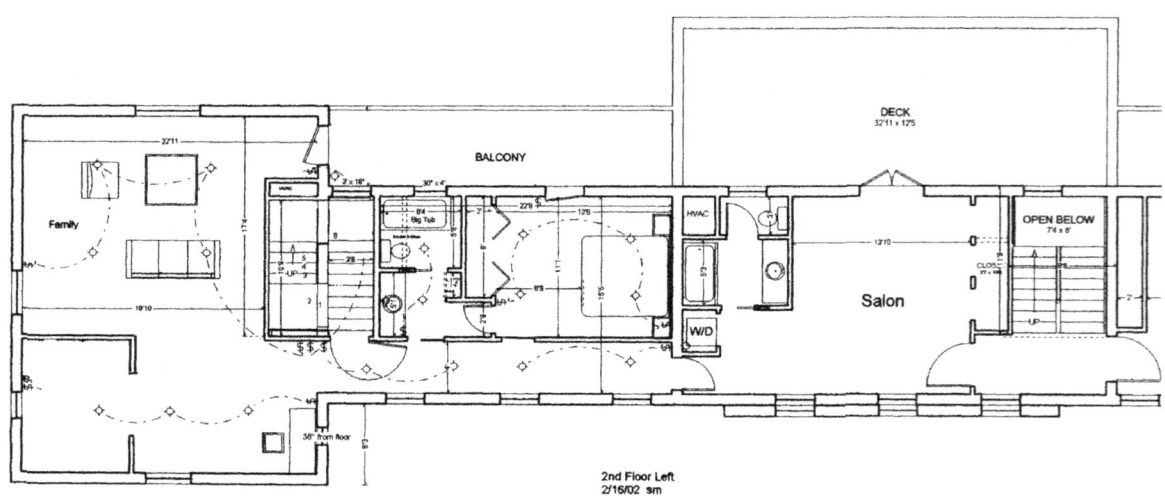

Figure 5-5b: Second floor plan

Phase 2 Construction - Left Wing

About a year after phase 1 was built and occupied, the designer completed detailed plans for the 3,000-square-foot left addition. Since many of the details for phase 2 had been postponed, there were a number of decisions to be made — footprint, room design, and stairwell. The architecture of this left side is intended to resemble the Norman chateau, but on a reduced scale. The left wing is approximately 26' long; and the left tower is about 25' long; see Figure 5-1a for the front elevation. On the ground floor there is a front side entrance to the left tower, which I copied from the Norman chateau. In Herbe, this door provides access to the garage, the stairwell or the study. My PC version of the floor plans for the first two floors is shown in Figure 5-5; the highlights in the phase 2 left wing are:

- Two-car garage - left tower
- Left tower front side entrance
- Study (15' x 23') - left wing first floor
- Family room (27' x 19') - left tower second floor
- Office or bedroom (11' x 14') and rear deck - left wing second floor
- Bedrooms (2) - third-floor wing and tower
- Stairwell from garage to second and third floors - non-invasive

Stairwell Placement and Design
Three options for placing an 8'-wide U-shaped stairwell were investigated: entirely in the wing, entirely in the tower, or split between the two. Since a minimum bathroom is 6' wide, putting the stairwell in the 24' wing would limit the upstairs bedroom length to 10'. Putting the stairwell only in the tower would make an oversized 24' study on the first floor, and reduce the tower room widths by 8'. I split the stairwell so that it uses 4' of the wing and 4' of the tower, providing a slightly oversized 22' study (Figure 5-5a) and a 14'-long bedroom and 8'-wide bathroom, as per my draft second-floor plan in Figure 5-5b.

This stairwell has an unusually tight design with a privacy benefit — you can get to the third floor without passing through the second-floor hallway. The floor plan shows the modified U-shaped staircase with four landings and two mid-wall steps. For structural stability, the tower is built with an interior load-bearing wall using 10" ICF blocks. However, this wall contains passages between the tower and the wing, since the stairwell is split. These passages have a 10" thick footprint in the wall, sufficient for a single stair tread; see Figure 4-5a for a photo of this wall and the matching stair step.

Lessons Learned: Provide multiple private entrances in a large building.

To gain more room in the garage, this stairwell is suspended from the second floor using threaded steel rods; there are no supports coming up from the garage floor. Thus it should be unaffected if the floating garage floor were to shift a bit. There is room for a 7'-high closet and the study's electric fireplace under the steps. We received a building permit for the phase 2 addition in October 2001. Table 3 shows the 16-month history for this 3,000-square-foot addition. (Our open house party was held in February 2003.)

Figure 5-6: View of study ceiling beams

Table 3:
Phase 2 History

09/01	Grading; pier placements marked
10/01	Building permit received; piers drilled
11/01	Cages built; concrete placed
12/01	Grade beam steel tied
01/02	Grade beams completed, garage floor set, floor joists
02/02	First floor blocks set; study beams set; first concrete pour
03/02	Garage steel set; second floor blocks set; second concrete pour
04/02	Second floor steel set; ledgers and joists set; steps set
05/02	Third floor concrete pour; left wing roof trusses
06/02	Balcony; windows; doors;
07/02	Tower steel tripod; tower rafters;
08/02	Rough plumbing; electric; HVAC
09/02	Interior sheetrock and exterior stucco
10/02	Interior finishing; plumbing; electric; roofing
11/02	Cabinets; painting; study ceiling; roofing
12/02	Painting; floors; finishings; study paneling

Study Highlights
The study's paneled walls and fireplace (Figure 5-15a) became a focal point of the chateau's interior design, so we contacted an interior architect, C.F. Michael Chan, featured in *Architectural Design* magazine, for professional guidance. See also Figure 5-17b. Several locations for built-in bookcases were considered, and we settled on two in the front wall only. In the floor plan the bookcases are treated by the framer like two windows, and appear in the Figure 5-1a photograph as two white panels in the left wing between the three windows. A centered 5' doorway with glass pocket doors on the left end of the foyer leads to the study. (The exterior door from phase 1 was saved and re-used in phase 3). The overhead half-round transom window from phase 1 stays in place. After having lived with that interior window for a few years, I like the privacy, but regret that the grids interfere with the view of the study from the foyer. In phase 3, I eliminated this arched window to the living room, and instead used arched pocket doors, as can be seen in the interior photo in Figure 5-14a.

Lessons Learned: Salvage and re-use building materials in later phases.

Study Ceiling
After miscalculating the dimensions of the trim in phase 1 (see Chapter 2), and upon studying the Norman chateau in more detail, I hoped to gain some height in the study by using structural beams. However, since I had to maintain a level floor on the second story (132" from the first floor), only six more inches of height could be squeezed out. I considered four ceiling designs:

- Regular joists and flat sheetrock ceiling (no beams)
- Coffered with 5' square panels (6" beams both directions)
- Eight parallel 6" beams (no cross beams)
- Eight parallel beams forming nine rectangular ceiling trays (25" x 15')

Although the coffered design is quite appealing, it is less authentic in Norman architecture than a parallel beam ceiling. The tray ceiling (Figure 5-17b) was a nice compromise and may have some historic justification. But what kind of beams to use?

New structural lumber tends to warp with weather changes; while old beams are attractive, they require inspection before they can be used for new construction. For this reason, my contractor chose 9"x12" laminated glued beams (Glue-Lams®). Seating the beam-ends directly into the concrete wall would have been more historically authentic, but the structural engineers insisted on attaching them to a ledger beam around the room's perimeter. An ugly steel bracket meets the beam at the ledger. This bracket and beam complicate the interior design finishing. The photo in Figure 5-6 shows the eight parallel beams, installed in front-to-back orientation on 30" centers; the 2"x6" cross members get covered. Laminated beams have a variegated appearance and aren't particularly suited for staining, so we painted the beams and ceiling trays. I'd have preferred a stained ceiling.

Lessons Learned: With beams, form vs. function tradeoffs are often necessary.

Figure 5-7a: View of phase 2 front

Figure 5-7b: View of rear tower corbels

Tower and Garage Beams

The tower is 12' deeper than the wing and its 27' depth extends 6' beyond the wing's front wall, as shown to the left in Figure 5-7a, and similarly beyond the rear wall. The garage is therefore 27' wide, with doors on the tower's left side, as shown in the floor plan in Figure 5-5a. Since the second floor joists must be supported above this garage, we considered several structural options for spanning this long distance: a wall within the garage, cutting it into two sections; heavier joists to span the 27' length; or a mid-garage beam.

The structural designer chose to run a 12" steel "I" beam down the center of the garage ceiling, left to right within the tower, shown in Figure 5-7a. This steel beam is supported on the interior end by a similar vertical beam; the other end is seated into a bracket connected to the ICF concrete blocks on the garage's front wall. The third floor has a similar issue, as shown in the floor plan in Figure 5-5b. Instead of splitting the second floor room in half with an interior wall to support the third floor joists, an identical steel "I" beam is used across the top of the second floor. To attach the wooden BCI joists to the steel beams, a sandwich of wood is bolted to the beam and then the joists are attached.

In the late phase 2 construction photo in Figure 5-7a the windows are installed, and the mansard roof is extended over the new left wing. The two bookshelves in the front study wall located between the ground floor windows are framed in the ICF front wall and show up as two white panels. The decorative vertical cut lines in the foundation are also evident. The seam between the phase 1 building and the phase 2 addition is barely discernible.

Soffits and Corbels

The Norman chateau has a tall, impressive tower, and Herbe's tower is about 52' tall. The ICF framing blocks are about 45" taller than in the wing, as shown in the front elevation photo in Figure 5-7a. In ancient chateaux the roof extends beyond the building's frame. Corbels and soffits are used to support this ~3' extension. However, Herbe's corbels are strictly decorative, although they appear to be holding up the soffit. In reality this soffit box (below the roof) will be affixed to a pair of ledger boards that are bolted to the blocks' surface, shown in the phase 2 front view in Figure 5-7a.

In the later rear photo in Figure 5-7b this plywood soffit box extends beneath the eaves, below which the corbels are attached. The plywood soffit boxes are built using 2"x4" frames that have one long side bolted into the ledgers on the ICF blocks; hence the box is supported on one side edge only. Each corbel is 10" x 22" x 24" and is made of extruded Styrofoam (described in Chapter 4), then wrapped with fiberglass tape for protection from weather (and birds). The corbels are glued and nailed to the blocks; then everything is treated with stucco. After designing and building the corbels, I found I'd made a miscalculation and should have spaced them further apart. Because projecting objects appear larger than the spaces that separate them, I now think spaces between the corbels should be 20% larger than the width of the corbels themselves. I haven't found any guidelines for corbels in architecture books.

Lessons Learned: Calculate three-dimensional effect of trim.

Figure 5-8a: View of steel tripod

Figure 5-8b: View of tower construction

Steel Roof Construction

A characteristic of the chateaux in Normandy is their very tall towers. Most of these tower roofs are so steep that they provide no utilitarian function and are merely decorative. As I was basing my Chateau Herbe design on a particular Norman chateau, the tower's look as in Figure 5-7b was a high priority, albeit expensive.

Structurally, a tower is like a sail on a sailboat, as it must be able to withstand very high winds. Designing for this "dynamic" force trying to bend the tower is actually more important than just building a structure to stand up "statically." Engineering of the tower was of paramount importance; it would also be a challenge for designers and the carpenters to duplicate the decorative corbels, soffits, dormer windows, and roofline.

To meet the dynamic forces, the third-floor tower required specially engineered welded steel frames. Each corner has a steel tripod, tied to the 45"-high blocks using hardened steel J-bolts set 16" into the block's concrete cells, as shown in Figure 5-8a. It was exciting to see the 85' crane drop the steel tripods gently into place to mate to the pre-placed J-bolts; see Figure 6-2. A rectangular welded steel frame rests upon the four corner plates (tripod top). A modified steel tetrahedron sits upon this rectangle. Rafter boards are bolted to the sides of the steel beams, and the remaining roof structure is built of wood as in conventional houses. Figure 5-8b shows the 2"x12" roofing rafters being attached to the tower, which stands 52' off the ground. Most of the steel was built off site, but the assembly and welding took place within the tower. The tower's 14' attic is unused. The wood frames for the soffit box are barely visible below the new roof framing.

The engineering for the tower was expensive, but the symmetry of the building offered the advantage that the next tower would be built using the same engineering design.

Also visible in Figure 5-8a are the small bolts extending from the tripod for attaching wooden "sister" members. When we built this first tower many of these bolts weren't really required, so in the next tower we eliminated the extra bolts to save some money.

Lessons Learned: Symmetry can save money in design and implementation.

On the other hand the steel fabricator had problems meeting the schedule and quality goals. Accordingly, I thought that on the second go-around, in phase 4, the problems would be minimized, and we would benefit from the learning curve of doing this project twice. I was wrong.

Lessons Learned: Abandon problematic vendors.

Figure 5-9a: View of rear tower

Figure 5-9b: View of steel deck support

Rear Second-Floor Deck

Phase 2, the left wing, includes a 6' deck at the rear of the building off the second floor, enhancing the bedroom as shown in Figure 5-9a. It overhangs the rear of the first floor's study, abutting the deeper phase 1 deck, and has a balustrade similar to those in phase 1. The two windows in the ground floor study are centered within the twin arches, and two partial arches are at each end.

This pan deck is constructed using a corrugated steel deck base, which is visible in the photo in Figure 5-9b. Concrete was floated upon this steel. The deck's beam is supported at both ends by the blocks, as well as by three wooden vertical support posts (Figure 5-9b). The deck's three scuppers feed into drainpipes that are attached and ultimately hidden within these vertical columns.

The second floor bedroom has a single wood/glass door to access this deck and the shorter bathroom window is partially concealed by the balustrade railing shown in Figure 5-9a. The soffit box has had decorative Styrofoam trim added, and the dormer window is framed and trimmed (also with Styrofoam). The rear slider door in the tower is installed. Some of the roofing is applied, and some ready for installation is sitting on the wing's roof. In the figures the dividing line between phase 1 and the not-yet-stuccoed phase 2 is more obvious. The 2' tall horizontal window lets light into the stairwell, and is also concealed behind the deck's railing. See the floor plan in Figure 5-5b.

Lessons Learned: Conceal anomalies.

Usability

After phase 2 was complete, the building had grown considerably larger, from 1,800 to 4,800 square feet, but the building also grew in quality. The two-car garage was very valuable because of the harsher winter weather. The garage also provided a large storage area above the cars. The study, with its oak wood-paneled walls, Brazilian cherry floor, and fireplace, provided a much warmer, richly appointed living room beyond the garden room, which had been playing the role of both dining room and living room previously. Our office desk was moved from the front foyer window into the study, and we completed the originally-planned guest closet in the foyer, as shown in the phase 1 plan. By adding more bedrooms and bathrooms, we more than doubled the living capacity within the house. The tower's family room was quite interesting, and the steep tower walls provided the most architecturally interesting room in the chateau, see Figure 5-15b.

There were no expansion joints provided in the pan deck's concrete, and this 30'-long deck has developed cracks. I think the single door from the second floor bedroom to the rear deck doesn't provide enough light into the room, so in the next wing I switched to a double door, doubling the glass area to improve the natural lighting.

Figure 5-10a: View of phase 3 right wing

Figure 5-10b: Rear view of right wing

Phase 3 Construction - Right Wing

During most of 2003 I reviewed and revised plans for the right wing. The major decision was to make the front elevation of the wings symmetric; consequently each wing has the same length and window placements. Many of the lessons learned from building the earlier two phases were incorporated where possible. In December 2004, 12 piers were drilled for the phase 3 right wing, but the right tower design was delayed for both financial and design reasons, and the tower would become the fourth phase of my construction project.

Lessons Learned: You may have more building phases than planned.

Construction started on the 1,400-square-foot (phase 3) right wing addition shown in Figure 5-10a, adding the living room to the right of the foyer, and two more bedrooms and bathrooms upstairs. Since these two bedrooms were accessible from the existing (phase 1) stairwell, they would be immediately usable. On the other hand, the living room wouldn't be connected until the new kitchen was added, and the old kitchen was changed into a wet bar, so we delayed finishing the living room-- synchronized with the right tower addition.

Lessons Learned: Some additions are more time critical than others.

Rear Symmetry Lost

Although I generally adopted a top-down view of the design, letting the exterior window placement dominate the floor-plan decisions, I decided to be more flexible on the rear elevation, and allowed differences. As a result of the window placement at the rear of the living room, the arches behind these windows are different from those in the rear of the study. Accordingly, the right wing has three full 8' arches, as shown in Figure 5-10b, rather than the two larger arches behind the study, shown in Figure 5-9a. The two sets of arches are far enough apart that their size difference isn't noticeable to a casual observer.

Lessons Learned:
- Architectural differences aren't always noticeable.
- Changing window locations may have ramifications.

The upper two floors each have a bedroom and bath. The second-floor bedroom has a rear deck that provides the overhang for the three arches. Note that the shorter window serves the bathroom, but the eventual deck wall will conceal the anomaly of the windows' height differences. A centered pair of French doors provides light and deck access for this second-floor bedroom, shown in Figure 5-10b, representing a lesson learned from the phase 2 bedroom that had only a single door, Figure 5-9b.

Note the future phase 4 tower, which would eventually intrude into the third floor dormer area, sets the location of the outermost window, as in Figure 5-9a. As I wanted the windows in the new wing to be vertically aligned, the entire run of arches was moved 1' to the right.

Lessons Learned: Vertical alignment may be more important than horizontal symmetry.

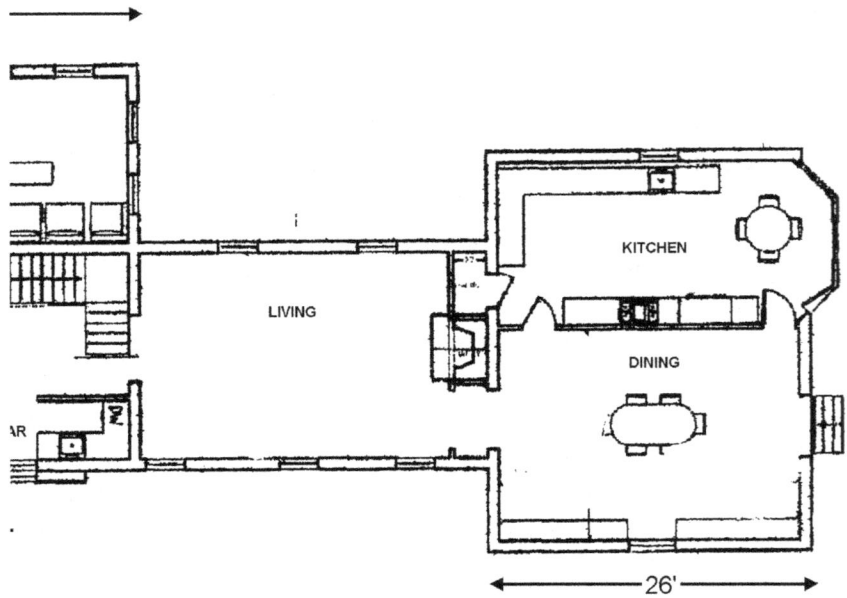

Figure 5-11a: Floor plan right wing – original

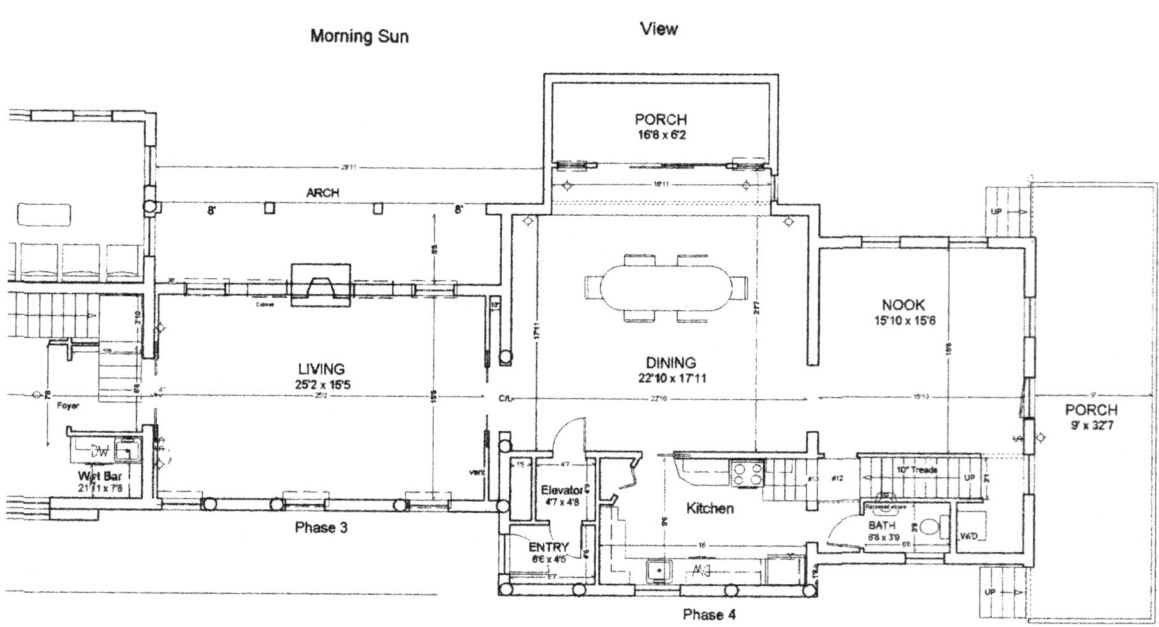

Figure 5-11b: Floor plan right wing – revised

Right Wing and Tower Design
Although symmetry was paramount in my early plans for the right wing, the multiple-phased implementation allowed me to make changes to my original concept described in Chapter 2 and shown in Figure 5-11a. The major changes, shown in Figure 5-11b, are:

- Adding a nook and porch at the end, breaking the symmetry
- Exchanging the dining room and kitchen locations
- Locating the living room fireplace on the rear wall
- Adding a side entrance, elevator, stairwell, and powder room
- Splitting the implementation into two phases

Lessons Learned: Phased implementation allows changing/improving your floor plan.

Living Room Design
My architectural advisors suggested a longitudinal axis running all the way through the living and dining rooms and out the tower on the right-hand side. Because I feared a visual tunneling effect, my original design did not have this long 80' path. Although torn, I decided to go with the professionals rather than my intuition. As a result, I moved the planned fireplace to the center of the rear living room wall rather than the end of the room. An interior designer (D. Siljak) suggested built-in cabinets adjacent to the fireplace, with the windows on each side, as shown in Figure 5-14b. Thus the windows in the rear of the living room are placed differently than those in the study; the rear of the building isn't as symmetric as the front. The rear arches are also affected.

After living in phase 2, I regretted using a window over the study's pocket door, because its grids interfere with the view of the study from the foyer. I fixed this problem when designing the living room's pocket doors. The archways use a pair of rectangular doors, 110" tall, that give the illusion of an arched door pair when closed, see Figure 5-14a. When the doors are open, there is an unobstructed view through the archway (no window framing). These pocket doors are in thick walls that shorten the living room by 2' on both ends, but these very thick interior walls add to the authentic character of the chateau, Figure 5-11b.

Lessons Learned: Consider the view, even for interior doors.

Little structural engineering was required for the right wing as it mirrored the left side; except the dining room/kitchen 6" structural wall eliminates the need for a steel beam as was used in the garage tower. The piers were set, as in Figure 4-1a, and after the permit was received in January 2004, the concrete grade beam and piers were poured all at once, rather than in two steps as previously. Because of the symmetry, we re-used the phase 2 left foundation forms for the right foundation, again saving money. Figure 5-12a shows the central section easily extended to the right with two end doorways framed for connection to the future phase 4 tower. The mansard roof is easy to extend over the right wing.

Lessons Learned:
- Symmetry can save money in design and material.
- Design roofs that are easy to extend.

Figure 5-12a: View of right wing framing

Figure 5-12b: View of living room steel ceiling joists

Living Room Ceiling - Steel Beams

I considered various options to gain some ceiling height in the first-floor living room, as my original choice of 10' for the ground floor is not as bold as most chateaux. One idea was to raise the second floor in the right wing by a foot, but since the exterior window locations need to be the same on both sides of Chateau Herbe, this would position the windows too low inside the bedrooms. Instead, I chose to squeeze a few inches out of the living room ceiling, as I had also done in the left wing study, and to leave the second floor position in the right wing the same as on the left. See Figures 5-14 for photos of the living room.

A normal BCI ceiling joist is 12" tall, but to gain some more ceiling height in the living room, I chose novel 4" rectangular steel tubing as ceiling joists. See Figure 5-12b for a view of these joists. The archway is at the building's exterior end. These 1/4"-thick steel beams on 16" centers are welded to angled steel "L" bracket ledgers around the room perimeter. This yielded about 7" of additional living room ceiling height, however the smaller ceiling cavity aggravates installing lighting and plumbing traps! This design required some new structural engineering, and even though the span is only 16', the engineer suggested steel center stiffeners for the ends of the ceiling, as can be seen in the photo. However, to attach sheetrock on the ceiling we had to "sister" wood members adjacent to the steel beams.

Lessons Learned: Gaining a few extra inches can be expensive; plan ahead.

The bedrooms and baths were ready for use after about 10 months, as indicated by the detailed schedule below. I chose inexpensive fiberglass showers, but fancier glass shower doors. The living room finishing was postponed.

Table 4:
Phase 3 Schedule 2004

01/04	Permit received, foundation framed, poured and stripped
02/04	First floor sheeting, first floor blocks, steel ledgers set First floor concrete poured, second floor sheeting
03/04	Second floor blocks, third floor sheeting, second concrete pour Gambrel beams and mansard rafters installed
04/04	Scissor rafters, roof sheeting and tarpaper, dormer windows set Interior framing, windows seated, balcony framed
05/04	Plumbing for two bathrooms (fiberglass showers)
06/04	Electrical for three floors
07/04	HVAC, sheetrock
08/04	Sheetrock taping, texturing, interior doors, cabinets
09/04	Bathroom lavatories, trim, painting, plumbing and electric finish
10/04	Wallpaper, carpet and lighting
11/04	Balcony balustrade
12/04	Living room finishing — postponed till phase 4

Figure 5-13a: View of rear nook and dining room

Figure 5-13b: View of Chateau during phase 4

Phase 4 Construction - Right Tower and Nook

Originally I planned to build the entire right wing and tower all at once, but as a compromise divided the project in two, phase 3 and phase 4. The tower/phase 4 building permit was received in June 2004, while construction of the 22 piers was in progress. Due to the driller's other projects, the piers took more than a month to get placed. I had decided to add a single-story nook at the end of the building, so the total square footage for this addition was 2,500. Although the building would not be symmetrical, I thought the small, single-story nook would be an interesting addition. I had seen such a building in a residential neighborhood outside Philadelphia, and also several photos in architecture books about Platt and Lindberg. A photo of the rear elevation showing the nook on the left with deck above, and the wooden dining room bump-out is in Figure 5-13a.

Dining Room Bump-Out

I had decided to bump out the rear of the dining room in the tower by about 3' to gain some room size, and for internal dramatic effect. Two options were considered: a rounded bay window using five 36" identical single doors, or a rectangular bump-out. Professionals, concerned at adding yet another design element (curved), preferred the rectangular bump-out shown in Figure 5-13a as being less obtrusive in the exterior elevation. For structural reasons, the bump-out is 17' wide with a steel beam over the doorway.

Since the best views are in the rear, to gain more glass I used sliding glass doors. Although not as traditional as French doors, sliders are less expensive. Standard door heights are 84", but they are also available (40% more expensive) in 96"-tall versions, which I used. Another compromise was to set these doors 6" off the floor to gain a little bit more visibility at the tops of the doors. The disadvantage is that you need to step up and over the threshold to pass through the doors. For the rear 3' bump-out, I chose a 10' wide slider with four panels, and a pair of adjacent fixed windows, (Figure 5-13a).

Front Elevation

Figure 5-13b is a late phase 4 photo showing the almost-completed building. The deck at the right end of the nook is not yet in place, nor is the right lawn. The pond and bridge in the foreground define the entrance to the "estate," and the driveway takes a 40-degree bend to the right after the bridge, as described in chapter 3. The new vineyard is partially visible.

As a chateau is usually a fortified building, it truly needs some sort of defensive structure. In ancient times a moat and drawbridge served this purpose. As chateaux are modernized, the drawbridge is usually replaced by a fixed bridge, and the moat might either be filled in or drained. In the case of chateau Herbe, the bridge shown in Figure 5-13b is just representational of a real bridge, and the ponds serve as a reminder of a possible water source for a moat. The bridge is actually just a driveway with side rails. Three culverts under this roadway allow the flow of water from the upper ponds to the lower pond to the right that is not shown in this photo. The ponds are continuously fed from an irrigation canal above my property, and the water flows through the three ponds and then through an underground culvert to the creek, beyond the tree line at the top right of the photo.

Figure 5-14a: View of living room door panels

Figure 5-14b: View of living room fireplace and cabinets

Right Wing Stairs and Elevator
My original plan did not call for a stairwell in the right wing, as the central steps were to be used. I added a right-wing stairwell to get to the second floor above, and also added an elevator in the tower (see below). The nook and dining room were built in Phase 4.

For about $35k it was feasible to put in an elevator with four stops — the exterior ground floor (35" lower than the first floor), and the three construction floors. The footprint of the elevator is about 5'x5' and is pretty efficient compared with a stairwell; see Figure 5-11b for its location. However, its placement needs to be towards the front of the building, which squeezes the rooms in the front corner of the tower-- the kitchen and upstairs bathrooms. The elevator is convenient for a B&B or to facilitate handicapped access to the building.

Table 5
Phase 4 Schedule 2004/2006

06/04 Permit received
08/04 All piers drilled and set
09/04 Pour foundation and piers, first floor sheeting, and first floor blocks
10/04 Pour first floor blocks, second floor sheeting and second floor blocks
11/04 Pour second floor blocks, frame interior walls
12/04 Form tower steel, frame dining room rear door/window
01/05 Frame tower, install windows
02/05 Sheet tower, frame third floor interior, corbels, rough plumbing
03/05 Plumbing top out, rough HVAC, balustrades/wall caps, electrical
04/05 Electrical, exterior stucco
05/05 Interior sprinkler (delayed), insulation, nook patio concrete
07/05 Sheetrock taping and texture
08/05 Cabinets, trim, priming and painting
09/05 Cabinets, painting, elevator, decking
10/05 Plumbing, electric, painting
11/05 Tile, doors, painting
12/05 Tile, counter tops, painting and finishing
01/06 Painting, built-ins, lighting, plumbing

A construction boom in the Ashland area during the 2004/2005 period made it much more difficult to get subcontractors' attention. Some of the specialists have little competition and the consumer must suffer delays. Major delays in this phase were from the pier drilling, steel tower, the interior sprinkler system, tile, and the nook's waterproof decking.

During the phase 4 construction we completed the living room, including arched entry doors, stenciled wall panels, and a traditional basket weave floor as shown in Figure 5-14a. The chair rail was set to match the window sills, at 24" off the floor, which is lower than standard, but it gives a strong horizontal line in the room and adds to the illusion of greater ceiling height. The living room fireplace and adjacent cabinets are shown in Figure 5-14b.

Figure 5-15a: View of study end wall

Figure 5-15b: View of third floor tower interior

Interior Design
In my readings and research I found little on the subject of interior design, but many books on decorating, so I learned a few things about moldings, panels, cabinets, window placements, and other interior-design issues.

Electric Fireplace
Most old chateaux needed multiple fireplaces to keep them warm, and many servants were kept busy just feeding the fires. It's interesting to count the number of chimneys projecting up through the roof in the photos of these old chateaux (Figure 1-1a).

Since Herbe has indoor forced-air heating and cooling, the primary role of a fireplace is decorative. As most communities forbid natural wood fireplaces in new homes, the usual solution is to install a gas-based fireplace with simulated fire logs. These also make excellent auxiliary room heaters; indeed their 25-40K BTU output can generate too much warmth for a single room such as the study. However, Herbe's site did not have natural gas as a utility, and adding propane just for a fireplace seemed extravagant. I chose a new electric fireplace with a simulated log flame, adding a separate 1500-watt heating option to throw some warmth into the room. Although the heater is not very fuel efficient, the electric flame bulbs are, and have both ecological and psychological appeal. Figure 5-15a shows the study end wall, the fiberglass fireplace surround and electric fireplace. A similar electric fireplace is used in the living room (Figure 5-14b) and in an upstairs bedroom. Also note the oak paneling and the tray ceiling in Figure 5-17b.

Entertainment Center
The stairwell in the phase 2 left wing from the second to the third floor tower requires a projection into the third floor for headroom for step #4 (to the landing), as in the floor plan in Figure 5-5b. A 20"-tall box/platform on the third floor was needed. We decided to build an entertainment center above this box, as shown in Figure 5-15b. This means that little space is lost on the third floor from this half of the split stairwell. The HVAC ducts run vertically up the left side of this unit and are hidden.

Base Moldings
Figure 5-15b shows a perimeter 12" base molding and a built-in bookcase on the right, and the entertainment center on the left within the third-floor chateau tower. Since many of my walls were 10" thick (Rastra ICF block), some of the framed interior walls were correspondingly thick. In this case we built a bookcase within a 10" stick-framed wall. Here a simple molding defines the bookcase exterior but runs right into the base molding. Had we raised the bookcase a little we would have avoided this merge. As this is the third floor in the tower, the ceiling begins to slope, corresponding to the roofline, above a point that is ~50" off of the floor.

Lessons Learned: Frame bookcases and displays.

Figure 5-16a: View of third floor tower rear window

Figure 5-16b: View of door and window moldings

Slider Window

Figure 5-16a shows a 5' slider door being used as a window to the third-floor balcony. Most of my ceilings were 10' tall, as described earlier. Standard door heights are 6½', which cuts off the top 2½' (best) view. Accordingly, an 8'-tall sliding door was more desirable, but costs almost twice as much as a standard slider. As the view and economy were both important, standard sliders were raised 9" off the floor, as shown. Note in the photo that the bottom of the slider's doorframe nearly matches the base molding height.

Lessons Learned: Raise sliders for a better view

Door and Window Surrounds

Molding surrounding doors and windows are usually 2"-5" wide, as shown in this corner photo, Figure 5-16b. It can be annoying if the window's top molding is not aligned with the door's molding when they are in close proximity. Since the door top is fixed in the floor plan, you need to frame the window such that its top lines up with the top of the door. If you miss by a little bit, you can correct this after framing by widening one of the moldings.

Lessons Learned: Match window and door tops.

Figure 5-17a shows a door surround molding adjacent to a bathroom counter (lav cabinet is 20"-22" deep). The photo shows how the counter top overhangs beyond the cabinet front about 1". The 3" doorway molding is placed allowing ~3" of "reveal" to the counter top. My typical design therefore budgets 29" (22" + 1" + 3" +3"), adding 34" for the door and its hinge side surround, setting my typical bathroom width to 63" (29" + 34"), not 60". As the door surround molding is about ½" thick, it projects into the room and may interfere with the opening of the drawer. It's best to also oversize the lavatory's length in your floor plan by an inch of filler on each end. For example, for a 48" long lav, plan on 50" after sheetrock.

Lessons Learned: Oversize framing for cabinets and moldings.

Tradeoffs of Building in Stages

Building a home in successive construction phases raises some issues and almost always involves extra costs that must be taken into account from the beginning. In the case of Herbe, building on a rural site required major improvements to bring power, water and septic service to the site. Since there are high fixed costs to installing this infrastructure, building a large house all at once has certain economies of scale. (On the other hand, the high cost of the infrastructure may be what's forcing the owner to build in smaller stages!)

However, the marginal costs for adding more electrical outlets and plumbing facilities in an expandable house aren't very different whether done all at once or in stages. There are additional costs for permits and inspections, but the actual construction costs are similar. Certainly, when an exterior wall becomes an interior wall, the exterior finishing cost is wasted. In the case of Herbe, some additional costs were a result of the multi-staged construction, and others could probably have been averted with better planning.

Figure 5-17a: View of bathroom cabinet and moldings

Figure 5-17b: Mazors in the finished study

Electrical

I made a bad choice in placing the electric meter in phase 1 near the foyer rather than on a post in front of the future tower, to which it was moved in phase 2 (cost of mistake: $1,200); the power company insists on a visible location. Each building phase has a 200-amp circuit system and its own breaker box. In phase 2 we put in a box large enough to supply power for all construction phases in the garage. The breaker box for phase 1 was in the foyer.

We have a number of electrical outlets on the exterior of the building and additionally we have conduits leading to the bridge, the pump house, and for exterior lighting. Most of the circuitry is very conventional manual switches, but for the central corridor of the ground floor I'm using low voltage relay circuits to control the ceiling lighting cans. As the building was extended we simply added another parallel path to control all of the relays.

Lessons Learned: Design electrical system for the final build out.

Plumbing

In phase 1 the water storage pressure tank and the water heater were located under the steps. In phase 2 they're relocated to the garage — extra cost. Note that the strategy of building the garage first would have avoided this relocation cost. Based on our experience with the well's hard water, we added a water softener system. The original septic system was planned for a six-bedroom house, so tying into the waste pipes and adding additional fixtures wasn't difficult.

HVAC

HVAC systems don't scale very well, so multiple systems seem to be the solution. I ended up with a total of four separate systems. The three-zone HVAC system in phase 1 is scaled to that building. We considered using the excess capacity of the phase 1 system to heat the second and third-floor bedrooms of phase 2 only, but decided against it because it wouldn't be sufficient to heat the two large living areas in the tower. In phase 2, we installed another system in the garage. The phase 2 study is connected to the first HVAC system, and we needed to drill through the grade beam at the foundation to access the HVAC pipes (the other alternative being to drill through the wall). Better planning from the start could have prevented this drilling through the beam. Both phase 3 (the wing) and the fourth-phase tower have their own systems. In total we have eight thermostat zones.

Break-thru

Recall that the 3rd floor wings and center are stick-built with wooden gables and have gambrel beams as shown in the photo in Figure 5-18a. During the phase 3 right wing addition we opened up the newly sheet rocked third floor end wall to expose the door frame built five years earlier during phase 1 as shown in Figure 5-2. What a thrill it was to break thru to the existing phase 1 staircase as per my original expansion plan shown in Figure 2-8! That same day we knocked out the center stud, hung a new door, so that I could walk through these two connected building phases—a wonderful experience.

Figure 5-18a: View of breaking-thru to existing building

Figure 5-18b: View of exterior thermal profile

Crawl Spaces

As Herbe was built in four stages, it had multiple foundations, each of which created a separate crawl space. Recall that the grade beam is about 16" thick and 36" tall, and to create a passage from one crawl space to another would require placing a gap within this foundation beam, weakening the structure. Access to every crawl space required more than five different access points, mostly trap doors in the floors of closets and pantries. For rooms such as the living room, there is no convenient way of providing an interior trap door; an outside passage above ground at the rear of the house and under the rear deck provides access to the crawl space under the living room.

Lessons Learned: Design crawl space access for each foundation room.

Thermal Profile

I photographed the exterior front of the left wing on a cold morning to get an idea of the thermal characteristics of the Rastra block. As the building was heated on the inside, dew formed on the warmer spots on the wall. The nearly circular patterns are the Styrofoam cells that have about a 10x better insulation value than the concrete cells that surround them. The ground floor bookshelves also have a different thermal pattern as do the areas just below the first floor windows. The upper floor's window surrounds also are done with Styrofoam. The building was finished with a base coat of stucco, but no paint had yet been applied.

Wine Cellar/Cave

Many of the old chateaux are associated with vineyards and sometimes have caves for storing wine. I thought it would be "neat" to have a cave as an extra garage or for entertaining. During June 2004 we did some test diggings into the side of the hill and, with the help of a local geologist, settled on a site directly across from the garage end of the left tower. The interim purpose of the digging is to provide a parking pad, then a garage, and finally a small wine cellar. I set the goal of having a room 16' x 24', but the hill contained a large amount of granite and shale that was quite difficult to excavate. Using a large excavator machine, we notched a section about 12' deep out of the hill during four days of jack hammering. With a berm and other "faking", we should be able to create the illusion of a tunnel. This project is planned for completion in 2006.

Solar Electric

Thanks to the incentives of the state and federal government we installed an array of 60 solar panels for generating 10KWH of electricity (when the sun shines). Since we used "green construction materials" in general, the solar system makes a nice eco-friendly system. The 60 panels are installed across from the chateau, up on a hill, on 6 steel frames.

Figure 6-1a: Photo of Skinner and Miller

Figure 6-1b: Photo of Spurling and Banks

Chapter 6
Vendors' Comments

Alan Miller, Miller's Renaissance Landscape Design, (Coordinator for Landscaping, Herbe II)

Using Stan and Maurine's pictures taken in Normandy, I began my task of recreating the outside to match their photos. It continues to be a challenge. As the dream was becoming reality, the task became a part of my life's work. I don't believe I'll ever have a more challenging or rewarding project. (See Figure 6-1a for a photo of Mike Skinner, left, and Alan Miller, right)

The Day the Cat Was Freed
The weekend started like any other: reading the paper, doing chores — calm, relaxed and quiet. Then the call came. Mike Skinner, who was working with me on the landscaping, had a problem. Mike, in his always calm, no-nonsense way, proceeded to tell me that in his efforts to dig out a new pond, something had become stuck in the mud. No, it wasn't his truck. It was something not easily extracted from the muck; it was his D4 Cat dozer. "Oh, it's sinking, can you get here pretty soon?" Panic set in. What in the world were we going to do? Mike had said something about hooking up the backhoe and seeing if I could pull him out.

When I arrived, it was very apparent that we had real trouble. We hooked up the backhoe. First attempt, second attempt, third attempt — the Cat continued to sink. About that time, my wife, Mary, arrived to take a look. "Oh my," she said, "You really have a problem here, don't you?" She laughed at the two grown men, standing knee deep in mud, watching this huge piece of equipment slowly sink. "What a lovely piece of lawn art," she said. "I'm sure the Mazors will love it. Maybe they can put lights on it at Christmas; that is, if it doesn't end up totally out of sight." We all laughed. But soon the laughter was replaced with a renewed sense of panic. The Cat continued to sink.

Mike and I finally decided that it was time to call for HELP! I called an excavator friend and pleaded for his assistance. "Please, oh please, come." "Not a problem. I'll be there as soon as I can get loaded up." His arrival couldn't have come at a better time. The seat of the Cat was under the mud and the exhaust stack was slowly sinking out of sight. The big Cat began its work and before long the little Cat was extracted from the hole. None of us cared about the mess. It was time for belly laughter and total relief. The Cat was freed.

Figure 6-2: View of tripod installation

Don Murray (Site Preparation Contractor) on Pier Drilling

Over the centuries the nearby creek waters had formed an alluvial plain of rich topsoil that was ideal for growing hay but quite unsuitable for supporting a foundation, so an engineered foundation was needed. Using a conventional drilling rig, holes were drilled through the topsoil and into the sandstone beneath for metal pier casings. In preparation for drilling, a pad of hard shale rock was built upon the meadow surface to provide a working surface for equipment and materials. This pad extended out on all sides beyond the building's footprint.

The 24-pier phase 1 casings are 10" in diameter and 20' long. The drilling truck was carefully set up over each of the marked pier positions. The rig's hydraulic stabilizing jacks were dropped on the shale's surface and pressurized so that the 25'-high drilling derrick mast was vertically plumb.

A 6" pilot hole was drilled first followed by a second 11" drill. When the hole was at least 3' into the sandstone beneath, the drilling was complete and the drill removed. At this point the 20' casing was hoisted to the top of the derrick mast and pressed into the existing pier hole using air pressure.

When the casing was seated into the sandstone, a clean-out drill was run down the casing. Using water and air pressure, dirt and rocks were flushed out of the casing, thus leaving the casing clean and ready for concrete to be poured.

Drama entered the process on hole #5; the drill operator noticed that the earth and shale under the rear jacks were falling into the borehole, causing the derrick mast to lean at a precarious angle. What to do?

There was a backhoe contractor on the property. The drill operator ran to the backhoe work site and asked for help. The hoe operator brought buckets of earth to fill the holes under the jack pads. As soon as water and air pressures were again applied to the drilling bit, the new soil disappeared into the borehole.

By now the imminent possibility of the drilling rig falling over onto its side became more acute. Shale had fallen into the hole around the bit and would not allow the extraction of the expensive ($500) drill bit from the sandstone. The drilling rig was saved from damage, no one was hurt and pier #5 had an expensive base for the casing! The remaining piers were drilled without incident.

Figure 6-3a: View of foyer kitchen

Figure 6-3b: View of rear deck scupper spout

Elvin Spurling, Western Design
(Professional Building Designer, Member A.I.B.D.)

Our motto is: "If you can dream it, we can design it." As I walk through the wings of the Herbe building, I still recall the excitement I felt as I spoke with Mr. Mazor over the phone the first time. I've designed over 1,200 homes, and each one of these was somebody's castle. But now to design a true castle — that's a privilege that doesn't come along every day.

So many questions were flooding my mind. How would it look? How would it be used? When would it need to be completed?

I said: "Some might think that building in pieces is not very smart and too expensive. No doubt the overall cost is more than doing it all once but, this is not that uncommon. Just look at how many remodels and additions are done every year. The biggest difference is, we're planning for the addition now, so it doesn't look like one when we're done."

Design Strategy - Divide and Conquer

To conquer this building project we divided the building into sections. Each section would be built in its entirety before moving to the next section. Each one of the sections would have at least two uses — interim use for that phase completed, and final usage upon completion of all phases.

When drawing phase 1 we spent only minimal time sketching the following phases. After phase one was completed, basic as-built drawings were created, to document, for example, if different framing members were used. Likewise, a change in doors or cabinetry could also affect subsequent construction phases. During phase 2 construction, a great many photographs, notes and sketches have been created to better aid in subsequent construction drawings.

At the beginning of phase 2, we put more detail into phase 3 planning. I believe committing the vision of the complete project to paper in detail would be a must for all future multi-phase construction projects. Does this mean you should have complete architectural plans for all phases of the project before ever breaking ground? No, that isn't very practical, because if the project is to be completed in phases over an extended period of time, the construction plans may become obsolete before they can be used. Having fairly detailed floor plans and elevations (side views) provides a road map to keep the project on track in each phase of construction. For example, if there needs to be a door joining rooms in the next phase, it should be planned for, and framed out in the current phase, lessening the work required for the next phase. Another critical example is the placement of plumbing and drains. Not knowing exactly how that space will be used in the future makes it difficult to build structures in phases economically.

Figure 6-4a: S. Banks and R. Olney sawing 30" block

Figure 6-4b: Framing with block

Detours and Roadblocks

A detailed map is a necessity if we want to get to our destination. But, as with everything else, there will always be scope-of-work changes, unforeseen conflicts — or just a better idea that is bound to occur during the course of construction. At such a time, good communication is a must. Due to the distance between owner, contractor, designer and engineer, e-mail has been indispensable. By the end of phase 2, almost 1,000 e-mails have been sent and/or received. Having this tool we were able to send photographs, drawings, and product information, as well as pass ideas back and forth between all of the affected parties, in real time. It has also been a great tool in reviewing conversations, because everything is in writing. This helps reduce misunderstanding and gives a written record to parties who may not have been able to participate in a face-to-face or a phone meeting.

The Road Yet Ahead Is a Ball

So with phase 3 on its way, I again find myself each night just before going to sleep, visualizing the grand opening ball:

"It truly had been a wonderful evening; everything went off without a hitch. The architecture, decorations, music, meal and service truly gave a feeling of elegance that has been almost lost with time. As the last of the guests filtered out I couldn't help but think about the years of work and planning that had gone into making this night a reality. Moreover, what a fitting setting — I mean, if you're going to build a castle, what better place than Ashland, Oregon, home of the Shakespeare Festival. This castle is nestled down in a somewhat narrow valley with lush landscape all around, and a tree-lined creek as a backdrop on the west side of the property. Yes, truly a great setting."

(See Figure 6-1b for a photo of Elvin Spurling, left, and Steven Banks, right)

Pete Hedenstrom, Specialty Exteriors
Rastra Rep, Oregon

Stan is no doubt the only person in the U.S. to use Rastra from four different manufacturing facilities on one project. I believe the very first block delivered was actually produced in the Riverside (Energrid) plant. The rest of the block used on phase 1 came first from Mexicali, and then some from the Juarez plant (both formerly Rastra USA, now "Perform"). The latest Rastra block came from the (Eterna) Pima, Arizona plant. When you use Rastra on phase 3 perhaps it will come from yet another plant right here in Oregon.

Figure 6-5a: View of concrete pouring

Figure 6-5b: Close-up view of concrete in block

Steven Banks (General Contractor) on Using Rastra

Having been in the building trade for 30 years, we've taken on all kinds of work, from log homes to geodesic domes, complete restorations on historic buildings to residential construction. By far the most interesting project is Herbe II.

When I was approached to build this project, I'd never worked with ICF Rastra block, so this presented a challenge to my crew and me. I remember the block distributor telling me there was a learning curve with this material, and for guys who were used to framing with wood primarily, we'd have to re-train ourselves to think in different ways.

The first thing we did was to check the square of the foundation and to chalk lines to set our block in a straight line. We set the corners first, and ran a string line to keep the block straight. On the second course of block, we would check level on the blocks and if it was out of level we would use a cedar shim shingle pushed between the block from inside or outside to level the pieces. Our ceilings were 10' tall, so we could set 10-plus feet of block height and then build our ledgers to hold the second floor in place. We used 4"x12"s as specified by the engineer for the ledger beams and came up with a plan to "temp" a wall under each ledger until the block was filled solid with concrete. This enabled us to pump concrete into the cells from the second floor (see Figure 6-5). We poured in 10' lifts.

Getting the steel rebar in the horizontal and vertical cells was not an easy undertaking. Fortunately the ICF block can be cut with a regular carpenter's handsaw, and drilled quite easily. If we had to install a piece of horizontal, we would drill a hole in the corner of the block and slide it in. The engineer required an L-shaped corner of rebar to overlap 2' in both directions. In the same manner, we could simply cut a slot and install the corner piece. In the process of joining wood to concrete, we used more steel than in a conventional framed building, and we knew what was being built was solid.

Doors and window openings were unusual to us at first because we were used to nailing everything together in conventional framing, whereas here we found ourselves using semi-expanding foam glue to put the blocks together, and also to set window tops and trims. When at all possible, we tried to have poured concrete at side and bottom openings so we could drill in anchor bolts to attach pressure treated lumber, especially in doorways. This would give us wood to screw the door jambs into. Our windows were vinyl type, so we were able to glue ICF 2" stock inside and out as stops. This method proved quite effective. Our building site can be extremely windy, with gusts of up to over 50 mph. The windows are tight with no leaks.

After working with the block, we realized how versatile the material is for forming interior and exterior arches, door, window and decorative trims. While building phase 1 we kept in mind the interfaces for the second and third phases for making connections into the phase 1 building. Having completed Herbe I'd use ICF blocks all the time if I had the opportunity. The end result is a building that is both energy efficient and very pleasing to the eye in both the interior and exterior. I believe it will prove to be extremely strong and durable. (See Figure 6-1b for a photo of Spurling, left, and Banks, right).

Figure 6-6a: Mazors toast in Garden Room

Figure 6-6b: View of phase 4 construction

Karl Holik, Rastra Corporation

Rastra cavity blocks fall in the category of Insulated Concrete Forms (ICFs). I visited a European house in 1967 made of a pure EPS (expanded polystyrene), and that was my first encounter with an ICF. EPS mixed with concrete turns out to be better because of the outstanding physical properties of the material, such as vapor diffusion, fire resistance and the fact that it is vermin- and insect-proof. EPS concrete is easier to work with and does not need special preparation for applying plaster or stucco. This mixed material is superior to pure polystyrene.

ICFs have advantages over wood frame homes because of the built-in layer of foam insulation, making ICFs energy efficient with lower homeowner energy bills, and a barrier to external sound. Other advantages include resistance to extreme environmental conditions, fewer repairs, and a healthier environment. Because of the high thermal mass, day/night temperature swings can be put to work to help save energy. ICF homes have a proven track record of withstanding the ravages of hurricanes, tornadoes and fires. The Rastra system is non-combustible.

ICF combines concrete, a centuries-old technology, and modern concepts of green construction. Rastra is a true champion, using recycled materials to produce energy efficient homes. There is a worldwide emphasis in this century to preserving the environment; the demand for lumber used in framed construction is reducing many of the beautiful national forests. Rastra eliminates the use of lumber for framing. A 2,000-square-foot Rastra-built home, including ceilings and interior walls, will save approximately 32,000 board feet of lumber — an average of 10 trees. Polystyrene, the familiar plastic product used in packing materials, food containers, building materials and a broad range of other products, has always been of concern to environmentalists. Now Rastra provides the perfect final "resting place" for the polystyrene. More than 85% of the content of the Rastra products are recycled post-consumer materials.

Rastra received early approval by the ICBO (International Conference of Building Officials). Over the years Rastra has undergone more testing in the U.S.A., and meanwhile the ICBO has become familiar with ICFs in general and with Rastra in particular. Now Rastra and other ICFs enjoy full approval by building codes.

Rastra was well accepted in the colder and changing climate in Europe and because of its versatility, it has become a household name in the Southwest of the U.S.A. It allows architects and contractors to fully express their imagination and the playfulness of the local styles — from adobe to sandstone blocks.

More than 5,000,000 Rastra panels have been used on four continents. Approximately 3,000 projects have been finished in the U.S.A. — residential and commercial. At this time, there are approximately 50 ICF products on the U.S. market. Now the major issue facing the ICF industry is a matter of public- and private-sector acceptance. The pure polystyrene ICF needs more bracing, cannot be installed in strong winds, is difficult to plaster, tends to encourage condensation and mold, and may lead to problems in fire and under vermin attack. Rastra ICF (EPS and concrete) avoids all of these problems. Rastra has an obvious advantage in performance and quality over pure polystyrene forms.

Statistics indicate the general trend is towards sustainability in construction, as the codes get more stringent. We at Rastra hope to fulfill our vision: to help preserve a world with forests, with clean air and clean water for future generations. We care for our environment and provide sustainable, affordable, and energy efficient buildings to meet new standards and to use recycled materials or those that can be replenished.

Afterword
Looking Back and Forth

In the first century B.C., Marcus Vitruvius documented in his *Ten Books on Architecture* the design rules used in Greece and Rome. He suggests that like the human body, a building should be symmetric. His work, defining the classical tradition of architecture, was translated into French in the early 16th century; its arrival probably contributed to the introduction of this neoclassic architecture style in France. Many of the chateaux constructed thereafter follow these classic architectural rules. Neighboring Italian architecture served up practical examples and provided classically trained architects such as Serlio from Bologna, whose ideas foreign artisans helped implement.

In the mid-18th century Blondel penned the four-volume *Architecture Française*, continuing the tradition of Vitruvius while making things practical and functional. (How will a room be heated, and where to place a bathtub?) The creation of the French royal academy of architecture in the same time period also encouraged architectural study.

Architects of smaller city homes wrestled with the constraints of neoclassic symmetry. Rural property offered a better opportunity for building a larger home that could implement the neoclassic style. These villas and chateaux in the countryside were typically used as retreats for the wealthy French, who more often lived permanently in Paris (or couldn't afford a city dwelling). This was the opposite of England, where the wealthy lived in their country estates and kept retreats in London.

On the north coast of France, Normandy serves as a beach escape for both Parisian and British tourists. There are a number of resort towns on that coast, such as Deauville and Tocqueville, which are popular in summer. The nearby countryside attracted a few aristocrats who built villas close to these towns. With an eye on the very famous chateaux such as Versailles and Chenencoux, these "lesser nobles" sought a design featuring a broad impressive façade, but with a modest and narrow building.

Accordingly I'm not surprised to find that the particular chateau near Deauville was enhanced by a wealthy banker to achieve its current long and narrow look. However, the visitor is struck by the variances in architecture in this structure from the original left tower, to the more recent car garage in the front right wing. It's sometimes difficult to determine if a feature is the result of an accident or fine planning. The chateau is not symmetric, and consequently some find it more interesting; see Figure 1-1a.

Francophile architecture was promoted in the U.S.A. by designers Richard Hunt, Louis Coffin, and McKim, Mead and White. Charles Platt also designed several classic style mansions. As an amateur, I studied these American designers in the final design phase of Herbe — should it follow my original symmetric, two-tower, plan or not? Incremental design provided a choice and a chance. Finally in phase 4, six years after I had started my project I added a breakfast nook on the right end as I'd seen in a number of homes, including those of Platt. I hope you can benefit from some of the lessons that I learned in this project!

About the Author

Stanley Mazor has over 40 years experience as a computer architect, chip designer, and teacher in Silicon Valley. He has been a guest lecturer at Stanford, University of Santa Clara, KTH in Stockholm, and in China, Finland and South Africa. He has published three books and over 50 articles. He is in the Inventor's Hall of Fame, the recipient of the American Innovator Award, the Kyoto Prize, the Robert Noyce Award, the SFSU Wall of Fame, and PC Magazine Lifetime Achievement Award. He is an amateur architect who enjoys cooking, writing and travelling. See the article by John Markoff in The New York Times, 2/17/05, pg. F-5 on Chateau Herbe.

Reader Exercises

1. Create a phase 2 treatment for the phase 1 powder room 2'×3' window.
2. Design the right wing and tower second floor master bedroom suite.
3. Design a stairwell in the right wing to reach the third floor.
4. What is the kitchen pantry ceiling clearance in phase 1?
5. Estimate the phase 1 kitchen pantry door size and swing direction.
6. Estimate the dimensions and clearances in the phase 1 powder room.
7. Propose the phase 3 dining room floor plan with an outside entrance.
8. Estimate the stair configuration for the front/side entry to the stairwell.
9. Propose an interior design for the phase 2 study: walls, furniture, other.
10. Complete a phase 2 design for the third floor bedrooms and baths.
11. Propose a plan for a ballroom behind the garage.
12. Draw three views of a 30"x30"x10" ICF block; show cavities with dashed lines.
13. What holds the vertical rebar in place within the ICF block cavity?
14. Add horizontal rebar to the block's drawing in #12 above.
15. What lifts the horizontal rebar off of the bottom of the ICF cell cavity?
16. Re-design the block's horizontal cavity with an arch to lift the rebar.
17. Draw three different configurations for building corners — mitered, etc.
18. L-shaped horizontal rebar is used at building corners; how is this placed?
19. Describe schemes for connecting a horizontal joist to an ICF wall.
20. Describe a scheme for placing a beam end into an ICF wall without a ledger.
21. Describe schemes for connecting a concrete floor to an ICF wall.
22. Describe schemes for building angled (mansard) roof with ICF blocks.
23. How would you make a curved wall using ICF blocks?
24. Identify four recycling sources for polystyrene for making ICF blocks.
25. Propose a passive solar design modification for the Herbe design.
26. Identify areas of thermal loss given the Herbe floor plan and site plan.
27. Propose a landscape plan for the Herbe gardens.
28. Explain the code "MM" on the Herbe II nameplate.
29. Estimate the potential ceiling height in the third floor tower.
30. Estimate the headroom needed within the third floor tower over the stairway.
31. Draw a cross sectional view of the third floor roof and gambrel roof.
32. Design a mini-kitchen for phase1 compatible with a wet bar footprint.
33. Propose a design sequence starting with the left tower only — garage first.
34. Describe ways of gaining ceiling height.

Appendix - Vendors

Western Design	Prineville, OR
KAS & Assoc. Engineering	Medford, OR
Bill Hicks, Geologist	Ashland, OR
North West Hand Crafted Homes	Talent, OR
Ashland Fabrication	Ashland, OR
Superior Windows and Doors	Ashland, OR
Air Temp	Medford, OR
Kaylor Electric	Medford, OR
Economy Plumbing	Ashland, OR
Ashland Lumber	Ashland, OR
Miller's Renaissance Landscape	Ashland, OR
Fontana Roofing	Medford, OR
Pro-Kote Waterproofing	Medford, OR
Cummings Bros. Sheetrock	Central Point, OR
Bill Britton Stucco	Medford, OR
All-Lifts	Medford, OR
Specialty Exteriors	Prineville, OR
Rastra Technologies	Scottsdale, AZ
Eterna Building System	Pima, AZ
All Lifts, LLC	Medford, OR
Solar Man Company	Grants Pass, OR
Danmar Cabinets	San Mateo, CA
Chatelle Woodworking	Oregon City, OR
Architectural Façades	Gilroy, CA
STO (stucco)	Atlanta, GA
Insulfoam	Kent, Washington
Elk Roof	Dallas, TX
Boise Cascade	Boise, ID
Empire Pacific Windows	Tualatin, OR
Insulate Windows/CertainTeed	Valley Forge, PA
Best Built Windows/Atrium	Seattle, WA
Therma-Tru Doors	Toledo, OH
ClimateMaster HVAC	Oklahoma City, OK
Carrier HVAC	Syracuse, NY
Majestic Fireplace	Ontario, Canada
Brøderbund Software	Novato, CA

Made in the USA
Middletown, DE
09 February 2021